Classic Pathfinder 5

Learning by ear and by eye

Classic
PATHFINDER

You speak, they speak: focus on target language use
(CLASSIC PATHFINDER 1)
Barry Jones, Susan Halliwell and Bernadette Holmes

Challenging classes: focus on pupil behaviour
(CLASSIC PATHFINDER 2)
Jenifer Alison and Susan Halliwell

Inspiring performance: focus on drama and song
(CLASSIC PATHFINDER 3)
Judith Hamilton, Anne McLeod and Steven Fawkes

Doing it for themselves: focus on learning strategies and vocabulary building
(CLASSIC PATHFINDER 4)
Vee Harris and David Snow

Learning by ear and by eye
(CLASSIC PATHFINDER 5)
Karen Turner, Iain Mitchell and Ann Swarbrick

Patterns and procedures: focus on phonics and grammar
(CLASSIC PATHFINDER 6)
Heather Rendall

CILT, the National Centre for Languages, seeks to support and develop multilingualism and intercultural competence among all sectors of the population in the UK.

CILT is a registered charity, supported by Central Government grants.

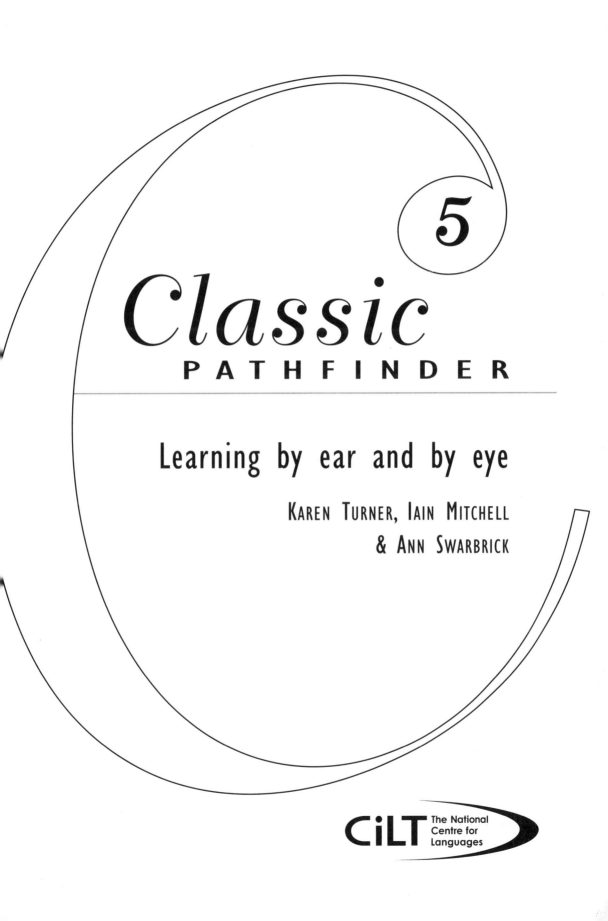

Classic

PATHFINDER

5

Learning by ear and by eye

KAREN TURNER, IAIN MITCHELL & ANN SWARBRICK

CiLT The National Centre for Languages

The views expressed in this publication are the authors' and do not necessarily represent those of CILT.

Acknowledgements

The authors and publisher would like to thank copyright holders for permission to reproduce copyright material, as detailed next to the relevant excerpts.

This compilation first published 2005 by CILT, the National Centre for Languages, 20 Bedfordbury, London WC2N 4LB

This compilation copyright © CILT, the National Centre for Languages 2005

Listening in a foreign language first published 1995; second edition 2005; © CILT, the National Centre for Languages 2005

Developing skills for independent reading first published 1994; second edition 2005; © CILT, the National Centre for Languages 2005

ISBN 1 904243 35 5

A catalogue record for this book is available from the British Library

Printed in Great Britain by Hobbs the Printers Ltd, Brunel Road, Totton, Hampshire SO30 3WX.

CILT Publications are available from: **Central Books**, 99 Wallis Rd, London E9 5LN. Tel: 0845 458 9910. Fax: 0845 458 9912. Book trade representation (UK and Ireland): **Broadcast Book Services**, Charter House, 29a London Rd, Croydon CR0 2RE. Tel: 020 8681 8949. Fax: 020 8688 0615.

Contents

Foreword

Learning by ear and by eye brings together the 'receptive' skills of listening and reading. It offers very timely advice as to how teachers can approach the development of these two skills, not only in terms of how to focus explicitly on the strategies of reading or listening with pupils, but also how to carefully select the material they use according to its level of difficulty and interest for their learners.

It is timely as, with the roll out of the Key Stage 3 Strategy for Modern Foreign Languages in England, there is an increasing focus on how pupils develop their linguistic knowledge and skills. The Key Stage 3 Framework of Objectives states that pupils in Year 7 be taught:

- how to engage with the sound patterns and other characteristics of the spoken language;
- how to improve their capacity to follow speech of different kinds and in different contexts;
- how to read and understand simple texts using cues in language, layout and context to aid understanding;
- how to assess simple texts for gist, purpose, intended audience and degree of difficulty as a preliminary to reading.

The key phrase of these objectives is 'how to …', since it demands more awareness in teachers of what pupils are being asked to do and requires them to share and discuss effective strategies with their classes. The authors of this book explore how we, as teachers, often over-estimate the skills that pupils bring to reading and listening tasks; that if pupils are not aware of what they are doing as they listen or read they are prone to making wild guesses or to being put off the task entirely. The authors propose a variety of activities that can enable pupils to be more conscious not only of their pre-existing knowledge and skills, but also of what strategies they should employ to improve their performance in listening and reading activities. Prediction activities, for example, can be used before tackling a task and encourage pupils to look for clues in the text type, in the situation or in the accompanying pictures so that they are better able to understand and learn from the listening or reading passage.

Another of the developments of the Key Stage 3 Strategy for MFL is the focus on modelling tasks, that is sharing with pupils the thought processes behind completing a reading or writing activity. In listening, too, teachers need to make informed choices about what they are expecting pupils to do as they listen and about the level of difficulty of the listening passage. In Part 1: 'Listening in a foreign language' it is made clear how support can be added or taken away from listening tasks to adjust the level of difficulty and how they can be differentiated to suit certain learners or groups of learners. Progression in listening skills is also encouraged, so that pupils are able to move from carefully structured exercises to more open-ended listening passages, containing more peripheral or authentic language.

In Part 2: 'Developing skills for independent reading', the authors look not only at how we explore reading strategies with pupils, but also how we select texts for different types of reading activity. Pupils need to develop both intensive and extensive reading skills. Reading intensively clearly has a pay off in terms of accurate language understanding, however reading for gist can be confidence boosting and can also enable pupils to read more interesting and complex texts, which can prove more motivating to some learners. There is also a vital cultural dimension that can be introduced through contemporary, authentic texts.

Both parts of the book look at how to find more motivating material either from authentic sources such as the Internet or from lively television programmes designed for MFL learners. For both listening and reading tasks we need to plan why we have chosen that particular material, in terms of motivation, and how it will fit in to our plan for the pupils' linguistic and skill development. The ultimate aim being that our pupils are able to be more independent when listening to or reading authentic foreign language material.

Ruth Bailey
Language Teaching Adviser, CILT, the National Centre for Languages

Part 1

Listening in a foreign language

A skill we take for granted?

KAREN TURNER

Introduction

LISTENING AND READING – HOW DO WE UNDERSTAND?

Listening and reading are often referred to as the receptive skills in contrast to the productive skills of speaking and writing. Successful listening and reading, however, still require our full attention. Making sense of what we hear and see involves both physical and mental processes, for what we perceive through the ears and eyes is understood by reference to what we already know. As listeners and readers we are actively involved in the comprehension process because, in order to bring meaning to spoken and written language, we must draw on information we hold in the long-term memory, the place where we store everything we know about the world. Understanding involves perception and cognition, the senses and the brain, doing and thinking.

The cognitive processes involved in understanding spoken and written language are of course invisible, which makes it difficult for us to know exactly how they work. However research where individuals 'think aloud' whilst listening and reading have provided psychologists with helpful data. The mental processes involved in listening and reading have much in common – the sounds and symbols we hear and see must be recognised as words we know which must in turn be organised into units of sense. At the same time, we must relate these units to what we already know which helps us to grasp the overall meaning of what the speaker or writer is telling us. Cognitive psychologists refer to these processes as 'bottom-up' and 'top-down'. Bottom-up processes are concerned with word recognition and top-down processes are concerned with prediction, interpretation, inferencing. In the field of reading there is a long history of dispute about the importance of one over the other, but current research suggests that the processes must work interactively and interdependently for comprehension to be successful (see Harrison 1996 for reading and Macaro 2003 page 155 for listening). If we rely too heavily on one process to the detriment of the other, either we fail to grasp overall meaning because we do not go beyond the level of words or we are prey to wild guesses because we do not (or cannot) recognise what the speaker/writer actually has to say. I will discuss the mental processes involved in listening in further detail on page 9.

However, having identified some common ground between the two skills in the way information is processed, we must also acknowledge that speech and writing are different in kind and some of the features of spoken language have the potential to make understanding more problematic. In particular, 'one-way' listening where the listener does not interact with the speaker to ask for clarification can present difficulties. In the foreign language classroom where extensive use of recorded material is the norm, listeners are also deprived of facial expression and body language. Drawing on Grenfell and Harris (1999), Rost (2002) and Macaro (2003), I highlight below some of the features of spoken language that have the potential to block the comprehension process.

- Spoken language is transitory and the speed of delivery is out of the listener's control, therefore word recognition needs to be very rapid.
- In continuous speech, words run into each other or may be shortened or may be completely swallowed up, making the identification of word boundaries more difficult.
- Intonation and stress are helpful but they are not as supportive as punctuation or the spaces between words in a written text.
- In spontaneous speech there may be incomplete phrases, hesitations, change of direction, variable speed.
- The speaker may have an unfamiliar regional accent.
- Listeners cannot move forwards and back through the text at their own pace to check understanding because oral text exists only in time so the whole is never available for perusal.

It is easy to see how both bottom-up and top-down processing might be blocked particularly if the subject matter is unfamiliar and there are unknown words. Listeners therefore need strategies for coping with the demands of understanding spoken language and these are discussed on page 28.

CHANGES MADE TO THE ORIGINAL EDITION

In the original Pathfinder 26: *Listening in a foreign language*, I focused in particular on the teacher's role in supporting learners through the grading of texts and tasks. In this new edition, I consider too the active role of the learner through a discussion of listening strategies. I make links with reading (see Part 2: *Developing skills for independent reading* for more about reading), relate the requirements of the listening component in national testing to the Common European Framework of Reference for Languages, provide more recent illustrative activities taken from published materials and update bibliographic references. The focus continues to be listening to recorded material rather than face-to-face interaction.

1 Listening in a first language: What can we learn?

In a first language, listening is inextricably bound up with speaking. In other words, it is through listening that we come to understand the world into which we are born and become an active participant in it. In the real world, we do not separate the skills of listening and speaking in the way that foreign language examinations do.

ROUTINES, RITUALS AND THE 'HERE AND NOW'

Babies are born with particularly sensitive hearing and are very soon able to discriminate human speech from all the sounds that surround them. In the early days hearing becomes listening – the listening out for and paying of attention to the particular voices of people who are special – mother, father, other carers. Long before children can talk, conversations 'without words' between carer and child take place with all the eye-to-eye contact and turn-taking of normal dialogues. Carers interpret as meaningful the noises and gestures of babies that take the place of a spoken reply.

Life at this stage is full of routines and rituals – being dressed, being fed, playing, having baths, going to bed – and the language of these one-sided conversations is rooted in the here and now. Talk centres on the concrete setting of daily life and home, on 'more milk' and the 'noisy rattle' or the 'soft puppy dog' where the spoken words are supported by the actual objects referred to. Well before speech emerges babies understand situations, that is, they make sense of what people **do**, and of course these situations are deeply embedded in a specific culture. What is more, what the speaker means is made clearer by particular stresses and intonations, by gestures and facial expressions. It's this understanding and knowledge of settings and events along with the language which accompanies them that allows children as they develop and mature to 'expect' and 'predict' both what is likely to happen and what is likely to be said in particular circumstances. What we know about the world, all that we store in the long-term memory has its beginnings in these early experiences of life.

'MOTHERESE'

It used to be thought that babies learned to talk by listening to normal adult conversation. Research has shown that many adults 'tailor' their speech for children. As we have seen above, their talk is focused on what is happening right now or on what happens regularly, but it also tends to be simplified – clearly enunciated with plenty of repetition. Sentences are short and structurally simple. Exaggerated intonation and stressed key words help to draw attention to the most important bits of what is being said. Just as important as this specially selected talk is the fact that children enjoy the undivided attention of the mother (or other prime carer) in one-to-one situations. As they begin to take a more active role in conversations, that is as they begin to use words rather than noises and gestures, meaning is sorted out between the two participants. Each listens to the other and the successful outcome is mutual understanding. However, the here and now – the situation – continues to support the words, so understanding what is meant is not so much the result of a close analysis of the words themselves but rather the result of the embeddedness of those words in a familiar context. As children continue to produce more language, moving from single words to phrases to sentences, the focus throughout is on meaning, making clear to others what they want to do, what they want to have, where they want to go and, along with learning how to mean, children acquire, without any awareness, the rules governing the language – its grammar.

In listening to a first language then, we can say that understanding is made easier by:

- a familiar and predictable environment;
- the undivided attention of adults in one-to-one situations;
- language which is tailored to suit the listener;
- gestures and expressions which accompany the words themselves.

WHEN THE GOING GETS HARDER

Young children are skilful listeners. In familiar and friendly settings when they are interacting with adults and peers and the talk is of a social nature, they are competent and successful. Children will listen to others, wait their turn in conversations, keep the talk going. In fact, the process of understanding and learning a first language seems pretty effortless for almost everyone. However, when the setting becomes more formal and the talk centres on the relaying of new information rather than on the social and interactional, children are not always so skilful. At school, for example, they have to listen much more closely to the teacher's words rather than relying on a rich, supportive environment to make things clear. This sort of listening calls upon **cognitive** skills rather than **social** ones, and it is in these situations that children are not always so competent. For example, some young children do not readily recognise ambiguous or inadequate messages. Because they are not accustomed to paying close attention to actual words, they either guess from experience what they think is meant or they believe it is their fault that they cannot understand. Good listeners are able to pinpoint what they have not understood and can say what it is that they need more information about. They are pro-active in the listening process and are able to identify what it is they need help with.

Listening is a skill that **develops over time** and children can be helped to get better. Recognition of the need to develop listening skills can be found in current government strategies for the primary and lower secondary schools. The DfES document, *Speaking, listening, learning* (2003) recommends that primary school children be **taught** to listen with sustained concentration and **taught** to ask for help and clarification. The *Key Stage 3 National Strategy Framework for teaching English* (DfEE 2001) states that 11–14 year-olds should be taught to recognise and later to reflect on and evaluate their own listening skills and strategies in different contexts. This assumes they have skills and strategies which may, in fact, **not** be the case. Nevertheless, the acknowledgement that listening has to be taught is welcome.

Understanding the mental processes

Understanding spoken language is inextricably bound up with memory. Researchers (see Rost 2002: 69–71, for example) suggest that the memory consists of several components which perform different functions. The short-term memory, associated with the here and now, includes an echoic memory which holds a brief, sensory afterimage of what has been heard, a sort of echo, and a working memory where we work on what has been heard by identifying words, making units of sense and creating links to what we already know. Grabe and Stoller (2002) suggest that the term 'working memory' is now preferred to 'short-term memory'. The long-term memory is where we store our knowledge of the world. We draw on existing knowledge to make sense of what we hear and we adapt it in the light of new information. The flow of information between the short- and long-term memory is two-way. In making sense of what we hear, we are constantly drawing on the knowledge we already hold.

The **short-term (working)** memory has strict limitations:

- it can only hold about seven items of information. These might be a series of numbers making up a telephone number, seven objects or groups of objects. The more meaningful the relationship between the items, the more we can hold on to;
- it can only hold on to these items of information fleetingly, between 10 and 20 seconds. To hold on to the information for longer, we must 'rehearse' it – say it out loud for example. This, of course, diverts attention away from the stream of sound which continues to come in through the ears.

The **long-term** memory has no such limitations. However, successful retrieval of information depends on how efficiently we have stored the knowledge we keep there. Efficient storage in turn is reliant upon the meaningfulness of the information to each individual.

The interaction between sound perception and mental processes is complex. This is what appears to happen when we listen and understand. We:

- take in a 'stream of sound', retaining it fleetingly in the echoic memory – some two seconds according to Rost (2002: 70);
- attempt to organise it into segments or chunks in the working memory – that is, to divide up the stream of sound into identifiable units of meaning. This includes recognising individual words. The stress and intonation of the speaker can help here;
- hold on to the units of meaning in the working memory and make a more detailed inspection, seeking the relationship between units, rejecting what seems redundant and holding on to what seems relevant;

- review what we hear in the light of what we already know by reference to the information we hold in the long-term memory;
- continue to take in more information through the ears;
- store the **meaning** of what we have heard (not the actual words) in the long-term memory if it seems appropriate.

These processes take place simultaneously, not sequentially, so we can appreciate that listening can carry a heavy 'cognitive load'.

The illustration below will clarify the process.

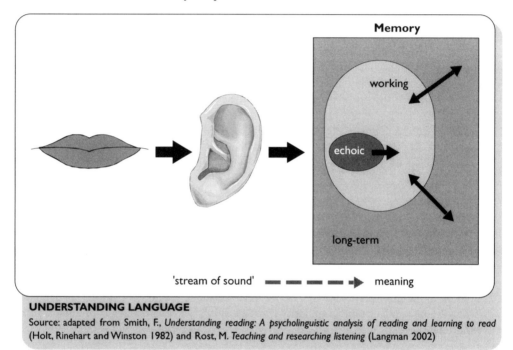

UNDERSTANDING LANGUAGE
Source: adapted from Smith, F., *Understanding reading: A psycholinguistic analysis of reading and learning to read* (Holt, Rinehart and Winston 1982) and Rost, M. *Teaching and researching listening* (Langman 2002)

HOW WE COPE WITH THE DEMANDS OF LISTENING

As we get older and become more knowledgeable, we are able to call upon our stores of knowledge to help us to understand spoken messages. We have a vast store of 'background' knowledge about social contexts which leads us to expect people to do and say certain things in particular situations. This is true for a whole range of settings from waiting in the doctor's surgery to socialising with friends. We are not surprised in the former if the person sitting next to us makes a comment about the weather or about how long you always have to wait for your turn.

This background knowledge helps us to make sense of a spoken message which is incomplete – perhaps a loud noise drowned out some of the words – or to drift in and out of a discussion where we are on familiar territory. We know enough about the subject matter to make sense of what is being said without listening attentively to every single word.

This knowledge differs for individuals. Knowledge about many everyday situations is common to all of us but what we 'know' is the result of who we are and the sorts of lives we lead. Not everyone, for example, knows about booking into hotel rooms or what starters, main courses and desserts are. People have different sorts of knowledge of a more specialist nature – about bikes and skateboards, about music and books. Plumbers have different specialist knowledge from teachers and solicitors.

Alongside this socio-cultural background knowledge, first language listeners also know an enormous amount about their own language. They know the sound system, they know what sort of words follow each other. In fact, we have all experienced the situation where, as listener, we are able to say out loud the words the speaker has in mind before the speaker him- or herself. We can then, in a first language, call upon knowledge that is both linguistic and non-linguistic to help us **construct the meaning** of what we hear. We are not passive recipients but active agents in the listening process and the meaning we construct is shaped by our cultural and linguistic experiences.

However, there are still occasions when we might 'get lost' temporarily or permanently in listening to spoken language, even with our mother tongue. Any of the following could send the comprehension process into disarray:

- an unfamiliar accent – for example it takes me some time to 'tune' my ear to the accents of an American film;
- too many unknown words – I find it difficult trying to understand the plumber explaining why my central heating has broken down;
- a complicated sentence structure – for example listening to a formal lecture that is scripted rather than spontaneous, such as the occasion when Chomsky spoke at the London University Institute of Education;
- too little background knowledge – the FT Share Index is an issue for some of us;
- a densely organised message – see Chomsky above;
- a demanding task – taking notes in our own words whilst listening to a lecture.

We can say that understanding the spoken word in any language involves complex mental processes but that in a mother tongue we are helped by many extra-linguistic features – like the situation, the expressions and gestures of the speakers, the face-to-face contact, the undivided attention – and by the knowledge we hold in the long-term memory which we build up gradually over the years.

Nevertheless, listening is **a skill that needs to be developed** just like any other skill. Understanding spoken language becomes more difficult when the extra-linguistic elements are missing – when listeners have only the words themselves to rely on. This, of course, is exactly what happens in foreign language classrooms and I shall now consider how best to help learners develop listening skills in the foreign language.

2 Listening in a foreign language: How can we help?

We have seen that listeners in a first language are actively involved in bringing meaning to what they are listening to. In doing this, they draw on their knowledge of the world and their knowledge about language. In addition to this, their listening is often supported by extra-linguistic elements. When we compare foreign language learners with first language listeners, we can see that the odds are not in their favour.

THE LEARNING ENVIRONMENT

The supportive environment of first language learning is absent in foreign language learning. We do not learn the foreign language in context, where the surroundings support understanding. Rather, we learn it in a 'decontextualised' way, in a classroom far removed from the real world of the target language speaker and the concrete objects of everyday life. We do not enjoy the undivided attention of the teacher on a one-to-one basis. Moreover, listening is made even more difficult because much of what we listen to comes from the disembodied voice of recorded material. We cannot signal comprehension problems to the cassette player by a puzzled look or a request for rewording. We could say then that in listening to foreign language recordings, we have a sort of **double decontextualisation**, a sort of 'listening twice removed,' removed from both setting and speaker. This means that cognitive demands will be that much greater.

Knowledge about the world

Most young learners in England until recently have begun their study of a foreign language at age eleven. This is changing as schools introduce a modern foreign language into the primary school curriculum for all seven to eleven year-olds, in line with the statutory entitlement to primary language from 2010 (for details on the Government's *National Languages Strategy* and modern languages in the primary school, see **www.dfes.gov.uk/languages/DSP_whatson_primary.cfm**). Eleven year-olds have considerable knowledge of the world. Some of this background knowledge about social contexts can be transferred to new situations to help make sense of what is heard, but there will also be many missing cultural elements. Their absence will reduce the possibilities for prediction.

Knowledge about language

The foreign language learner has everything to learn – a new sound system, new vocabulary, new grammatical system. This sort of knowledge cannot be acquired in the way it is acquired in a first language. In a **first** language, no one explicitly teaches us the sounds and the rules of grammar; we acquire them subconsciously as we learn to use language for particular purposes. This takes place gradually over a number of years.

In a **foreign** language, the learning of the sound system and the grammatical system has to be explicit because of the limited time available to the learner in the classroom setting. Learners need this knowledge of the grammatical system to help them predict the sorts of words and phrases that will be coming. Moreover, as was shown in Chapter 1, when listening is unsupported by a concrete setting, listeners must rely on the words themselves to access meaning. This means that it is important that learners know exactly how the words of the foreign language are put together to make meaning. It is not sufficient for them to have some vague idea of what whole phrases mean when they are used in a particular topic. Some of our listening to recordings must be concerned with the presentation and practice of sounds, words and patterns.

However, having made the point that learners need to hear specific language items in isolation, comprehension difficulties are more likely to arise when these items are integrated into continuous speech which may also contain unknown items. Listening for some can be an 'acoustic blur'. They are unable to relate the sounds they hear to the language they know. The difficulty is as noted earlier, that once known words are integrated into continuous speech, they are much harder to recognise. The pronunciation changes. Word boundaries are less clearly defined, that is, words run into each other or are swallowed up. It all sounds impossibly fast. Anxiety about not understanding every word reduces listening effectiveness. Our tape work, therefore, will gradually have to lead learners from the text that is tightly controlled and clearly enunciated to texts which are more open and rapidly delivered. We shall consider how to do this later in the chapter.

To **summarise** then, we can say that listening in a foreign language is more difficult because:

- the support systems are missing; there is: no concrete setting;
- in listening to recorded material, there is: no facial expression;
  no body language;
  no negotiated meaning;
- knowledge about language and background knowledge are limited;
- opportunities to hear the language are much reduced.

We cannot, therefore, simply assume that learners will automatically be successful listeners in a foreign language. Learners will benefit from being taught how to listen. Hawkins (1987) has argued for 'education of the ear' whereby listening skills are improved through activities specifically designed to develop aural discrimination. Examples of these are provided in the following section.

Developing listening skills

Teachers can help learners to develop their listening skills in these ways:

- talking about the listening process;
- compensating for the difficulties;
- adopting a teaching, not a testing, approach;
- teaching listening strategies.

In the following sections, each of these points is developed in detail.

Talking to learners about the listening process

Here are five discussions we might usefully have with learners.

Firstly, we could ask learners to tell us about the sorts of listening they do outside the foreign language classroom and to think about how they cope with difficulties. This could be the start of strategy development.

Secondly, we could tell them something about what happens 'inside the head' when they listen to their first language and how they make use of what they already know without even realising it. We could, for example, tell them a story, pausing now and then to ask them to suggest which word/s might come next and asking them how they know those words could come next and why they think those are suitable words. We could ask them to compare how they listen to the television at home with how they listen to teachers giving them information or instructions. This of course could only take place in English. From these discussions, learners should come to realise that listening in a foreign language is not going to be like social listening in a first language. They cannot drift in and out of listening in a foreign language but must be more attentive, must listen more carefully to the words themselves rather than relying on other sources to help them understand.

Thirdly, from the outset, we need to talk about the **new sounds** that learners will hear and will have to produce themselves. Here are some words which are easily recognised in the written form but which require the learning of new sounds:

bus (English)	*bus* (French)
bus (English)	*Bus* (German)
soup (English)	*soupe* (French)
July (English)	*julio* (Spanish)

Equally important, learners need to hear **small differences between words** and to understand how the difference **changes meaning**. On the following page are some examples where small differences need to be discriminated:

ich mache	*ich machte*
les cheveux	*les chevaux*
llego	*llegó*

Hearing these differences is fundamental to teaching good pronunciation and to understanding messages. The revised National Curriculum for Modern Foreign Languages (1999) which became statutory in 2000 made explicit the need to **teach** pronunciation (see Programme of Study 2b), a generally neglected aspect of communicative language teaching. It is an essential **language skill** to know that changes in sound, once you have heard them, affect the meaning of what you have heard and are not simply a slip of the tongue on the part of the speaker. The aptitude tests that were developed in the 1960s and 1970s showed that aural discrimination, the ability to hear small sound differences between words, and in particular the ability to link sound changes to grammatical concepts (*die Banane ... die Bananen*: singular to plural), was a key factor in language aptitude.

Developing the skills of aural discrimination is part of the Government strategy for modern foreign languages in Key Stage 3 (DfES 2003). Aural acuity should be developed over each year of the Key Stage as can be seen from these teaching objectives for Listening and Speaking:

Pupils should be taught:

- how to engage with the sound patterns and other characteristics of the spoken language (Year 7L1)
- to begin to listen for subtleties of speech (Year 8L1)
- to begin to interpret what they hear from content and tone (Year 9L1)

Activities concerned with the 'education of the ear' mentioned earlier are designed to help learners with sound discrimination. The following are three examples from two different books:

In the first example (Source: *Equipe 1* (1998), Unit 1: *Départ*: distinguishing between English and French sounds) learners hear the following ten phrases on the tape and say whether they are hearing French or English:

Transcript

1 – Footballer Eric Cantona.
2 – *Le footballeur Eric Cantona.*
3 – *Visite Paris!*
4 – Visit Paris!
5 – *L'Eurostar et le Shuttle.*
6 – The Eurostar and the Shuttle.

7 – *Un café et des croissants.*
8 – A coffee and croissants.
9 – *Le château de Versailles.*
10 – The château in Versailles.

They listen first and then have a go at repeating the phrases getting as close as possible to the correct pronunciation of the French. This activity also draws attention to stress-timed English and syllable-timed French and the final unpronounced 's' in Paris.

English	French
V̲isit	vi/ si/te
P̲aris	Pa/ ris

In the second example (Source: *Equipe 1* (1998), Unit 5: *Chez moi*: distinguishing between similar French sounds) learners listen to the tape to see if they can **hear** the difference between *est* and *et*.

Transcript

Dans ma chambre, le lit est rouge et le tapis est orange. La chaise est bleue et rose. L'étagère est blanche et la commode est orange et verte. L'ordinateur est sur le bureau. La lampe jaune est sur la commode orange et verte. L'armoire rose est entre le lit et le bureau. J'adore ma chambre!

Learners then **read the text** and practise making the difference in sound themselves.

In the third example (Source: Hawkins (1987) *Awareness of language: An introduction.* Appendix A: Learning to listen: Recognising different intonation patterns) learners listen to pairs of phrases said ironically (I) or sincerely (S) and note whether the pairs are identical or different:

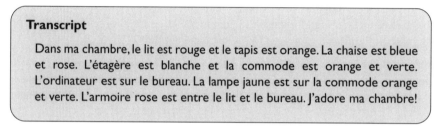

1 That's a big help!   (I) } different
   That's a big help!   (S)

2 That explains a lot!   (I) } identical
   That explains a lot!   (I)

3 Very interesting, I must say! (S) } different
   Very interesting, I must say! (I)

4 Thanks a lot!   (I) } different
   Thanks a lot!   (S)

5 Don't let me interrupt you! (I) } identical
   Don't let me interrupt you! (I)

Information is not always explicitly stated by a speaker. Listeners have to 'infer' opinions, attitudes and feelings. These activities can help with inference making.

I think that these activities work best where learners already know the words they are listening to. It's not difficult to prepare your own activities according to the needs of your learners. Beginners in French seem to find it difficult to discriminate between *je/j'ai/j'aime* so some listening discrimination on these could be very useful.

The fourth discussion that we might have with learners is more concerned with the listening skill itself. It is more psychological than physiological in nature. There is something about listening to a foreign language linked to our feelings of insecurity that makes us believe that if we do not understand every word, then we cannot grasp the overall meaning of what is being said. We switch off, give up. This is where teachers can help by setting tasks which direct the learner's attention only to those aspects of the text which are essential.

Lastly, we should impress on our learners the need to be **active** in the listening process by making sure they understand exactly what is required, by asking for repetition when necessary, by reading the questions carefully before starting and by thinking about the **sorts of answers** that are needed (how many listeners write down the time in answer to a Where? question!). These are the sorts of things 'strategic' listeners do – see pages 18 and 19.

COMPENSATING FOR THE DIFFICULTIES

The teacher needs to compensate for the missing support systems which we identified in first language listening. These were concerned with the learning environment and sources of knowledge that listeners might draw on. Compensatory measures take place before and during the listening activity. Pre-listening work prepares the learners for the listening activity. It focuses on setting the scene, preparing the ground linguistically and culturally and clarifying the nature of the task to be completed. Learners should not go in 'cold' to any listening activity. The tasks to be completed while the tape plays must be appropriate to the transitory nature of speech.

In the sections that follow there are some suggestions for the sort of work that might precede listening and some suggestions about the nature of tasks we set.

Pre-listening work

Preparing the ground

This is concerned with setting the scene, preparing the ground linguistically and culturally before the listening begins. As teachers, we should, for example:

- inform learners what the recording is about;
- provide a title and/or a brief summary;
- provide a purpose for listening;
- cover the key language items needed for understanding;
- indicate whether they will be listening to a monologue, a dialogue or a discussion;
- state who is talking to whom and give names if appropriate.

Any of the information we provide could well be displayed on the OHP or on the board for ongoing reference during the activity.

Setting the context allows learners to make **predictions** about the content of what they are about to hear in the way they would in a first language. Once the subject matter has been identified, teachers can capitalise on opportunities for the prediction of specific vocabulary and structures. Teacher-directed question and answer work, or a **brainstorming** by learners of all the language that comes to mind connected with the title, allows the recycling of what is known (or ought to be known!). This sort of work can be spontaneous with individuals offering words and phrases as they come to mind. It can also profitably be done in pairs or groups where some time for reflection and collaboration is available. Spellings can be verified together as learners make appropriate suggestions to the group. Preparation work such as this also provides the teacher with the opportunity to input new words that will be needed for understanding. By taking these steps, we are supporting both top-down (thinking about what is already known) and bottom-up (focusing on word meaning) processing.

Visuals or realia (props) can also be a useful way of setting a context, as can reading a short text together or listening to an oral summary by the teacher. It may well be that during this preparation for listening time the teacher will need to input some **cultural information** which will be essential if the learners are to be able to construct meaning from what they hear.

All the above provide us with opportunities for **clearly focused oral work**, the end product of which should be a supportive framework, possibly in written form on the OHP or board, for the listening task. Such activities are called 'advance organisers' because they do exactly that – allow listeners to be organised in advance.

Setting the task

Learners need to know **in advance** the task they are to complete. This creates a situation where listening is **directed** rather than it taking place in a vacuum.

Clarifying procedures

Before the listening begins, learners should be told how many times the tape will be played, whether the teacher will pause the tape at any stage to allow time for thinking and writing. This is psychologically reassuring – knowing that if the answer was not grasped the first time round, another opportunity is available.

Listening tasks

The tasks we set must be appropriate to the transitory nature of speech and take into account the limited capacity of the working memory. We can only attend to one stream of information or one train of thought at a time. This is called 'selective attention' (Rost 2002). Tasks that take too much time to complete deflect our attention away from making sense of the speech that continues to come in through the ears. In other words, we shall miss incoming information whilst we concentrate on recording what we have already heard. Suitable tasks will be quickly and easily completed and might include, for example:

- ticking boxes in a grid;
- ticking items on a list, not all of which will be included on the tape;
- either/or answers;
- putting in chronological order by numbering;

- writing figures or symbols;
- filling gaps with one word;
- filling grids with symbols or single words;
- correcting factual details, like colours, times, prices;
- making notes via key words – as, for example, in descriptions.

Many of these activities avoid the issue of whether answers should be recorded in the target language or not because they can be completed numerically or symbolically, so not only are they speedily carried out but time and attention are not wasted on thinking about accurate spellings.

It goes without saying that the layout of any worksheet or activity sheet must also acknowledge the fleeting nature of speech. A matching exercise which entails too much time searching for the matching items because they are scattered over the page will produce the same effect as an exercise which requires a lot of writing – it will divert the listener's attention away from incoming information.

In the example on page 20, learners must draw lines from the individuals speaking to the activities they are usually engaged in on a Saturday. The idea is good but the layout is unhelpful. It takes too long to link up the speakers with the activities which are randomly scattered over the page. The tape moves on whilst the eye must continue to search.

A grid of the sort we shall look at in detail later in the chapter (see page 26) would reduce the confusion of listeners, allow them to record the answers more easily and leave a more readable copy for feedback at the end of the activity.

Post-listening tasks

When the listening activity has been completed and answers checked, difficulties discussed and strategies shared, language work should move seamlessly on. Listening is not an end in itself. It is a means to an end – learning the language – so it must lead somewhere. Given the impoverished contact time allocated to foreign language learning in the English school system, one solution is to **recycle and consolidate language** through **all the skill areas** so that listening work leads smoothly into speaking, reading and/or writing. Some ideas are provided on page 26 in the section on Integrating the skills.

Hör gut zu! Was machen diese Leute am liebsten samstags?

Brigitte   Dieter   Natascha   Harald   Susi

ADOPTING A TEACHING APPROACH

A teaching approach is concerned with helping learners to develop their listening skills over a period of time. It involves:

- grading materials;
- grading tasks;
- integrating listening into the other skill areas;
- teaching learner strategies.

Grading materials

It is obvious from what has been said earlier in the chapter that learners need a wide range of different sorts of material with a varying focus. Rost (2002) usefully differentiates **learning to listen**, (i.e. understand spoken messages in the foreign language) and **listening to learn the language** (i.e. its forms and rules). In a first language, grammatical competence is acquired as a by-product of listening and understanding. In a foreign language, attention must be drawn specifically to the formal aspects of language because of limited exposure time. The distinction is very important for planning purposes but, of course, it is not absolute. Listeners must understand before they focus on form.

The grading of materials can be seen in several interconnected ways:

material	focus	language
pedagogic ↓	medium ↓	scripted ↓
↓	↓	semi-scripted ↓
	message ↓	quasi-authentic ↓
authentic	message	native speaker speech

Within any module or unit of teaching, and long-term throughout the duration of their studies, learners should progress in these three ways: moving from pedagogic material which is scripted, that is, carefully selected and sequenced, clearly enunciated and focused on teaching the language as a system, towards quasi-authentic material which is partially controlled in terms of content and/or speed of delivery and focused on the message being conveyed, and finally, in some cases, towards authentic material which is completely ungraded. By quasi-authentic material, I mean material that has been recorded with particular learners in mind, for example those preparing for the GCSE examination, but which has the appearance of being authentic, unrehearsed and spontaneous. An example of this would be native speaker adolescents answering specific questions posed by an interviewer in a fairly natural sort of way at more or less native speaker speed. I am classifying as authentic material which has been produced for **users** of the target language as opposed to learners. Recordings from national radio and television stations such as the news or discussions would fall into this category. Of course, with time as learners become more competent, the emphasis will move from the pedagogic and scripted to the more open-ended. Let us now look in more detail at some of these aspects of grading.

Pedagogic material

Good pedagogic material that aims to teach the grammatical system of the language (phonology, morphology, syntax) is clearly enunciated and spoken at a rate appropriate to learner proficiency. The pattern to be learned is repeated a number of times such that learners notice the repetition and can learn from it. The following is an example from *Equipe 1* (1998). The focus is the first and second person singular of the verb *avoir* present tense, used in conjunction with a range of nouns which could be presented visually prior to working with the tape. Known language (asking and giving names and ages) is recycled. There is a clear and appropriate context.

Example 1

Source: *Equipe 1* (Bourdais, Finnie and Gordon 1998), Unit 1: *Bienvenue*

Transcript

– Tu t'appelles comment?
– Je m'appelle Anne.
– Tu as quel âge, Anne?
– J'ai treize ans.
– Tu as des frères et sœurs?
– Oui, j'ai un frère.
– Un frère?
– Oui.
– Tu n'as pas de sœurs?
– Non, je n'ai pas de sœurs.
– Tu as un animal chez toi?
– Oui, j'ai un chat.

– Tu t'appelles comment?
– Je m'appelle Freddy.
– Et tu as quel âge, Freddy?
– J'ai douze ans.
– Tu as des frères et sœurs?
– Oui, j'ai deux frères.
– Tu as des sœurs?
– Oui, j'ai une sœur.
– Tu as un animal chez toi?
– Un animal? Oui. J'ai un lapin.

– Tu t'appelles comment?
– Je m'appelle Isabelle.
– Et tu as quel âge?
– J'ai onze ans.
– Tu as des frères et sœurs?
– Oui, j'ai une sœur.
– Une sœur, oui. Et tu as des frères?
– Non, je n'ai pas de frères.
– Tu as un animal chez toi?
– Non, je n'ai pas d'animal.

– Bonjour. Tu t'appelles comment?
– Je m'appelle Olivier.
– Et tu as quel âge, Olivier?
– J'ai douze ans.
– Tu as des frères et sœurs?
– Oui, j'ai deux frères.
– Tu as des sœurs?
– Oui, j'ai trois sœurs.
– Tu as un animal chez toi?
– Oui. J'ai deux perruches.

– Tu t'appelles comment?
– Je m'appelle Marine.
– Tu as quel âge?
– J'ai quatorze ans.
– Tu as des frères et sœurs?
– Oui. J'ai un frère et une sœur.
– Et … Tu as un animal chez toi?
– Oui. J'ai un chien.

– Tu t'appelles comment?
– Je m'appelle Grégory.
– Tu as quel âge?
– Dix ans.
– Tu as des frères et sœurs?
– Oui, j'ai deux sœurs.
– Très bien. Et tu as des frères?
– Non, je n'ai pas de frères.
– Tu as un animal chez toi?
– Un animal? Oui, J'ai des poissons rouges.
– Des poissons rouges?
– Oui, j'ai quatre poissons rouges.
– Très bien. Merci, Grégory.

The question and answer routine has a real life feel to it but to have all six respondents following exactly the same format is contrived. In a more authentic recording, there would be a variety of question and answer forms but this example serves its purpose well. Alone, this type of text constitutes far too restricted a diet; other types of texts are essential.

The next example is a Spanish text for more experienced learners. The focus here is on understanding messages. The language is more 'authentic' in the sense that the interviewer and interviewees use a variety of question and answer forms. A grid is provided for collecting the answers. The column headings direct the listener to the key information required. An extra box at the end of the row would be a helpful addition. Here skilled listeners could note any other information they understand from the recording. Such an **extension activity** keeps their attention focused whilst less skilled learners are listening for core information for a second or third time.

Example 2
Source: *Español a la vista* (Alonso de Sudea and Sookias 1998), *Paso 1*

Transcript

1 – Alejandro, descríbenos tu perro Lisi.
– Bueno, Lisi es de color gris y negro con ojos azules. Es grande y lo cuido mucho. Es increíblemente bonito.

2 – Y tú Elena, ¿tienes animales en casa?
– Pues animales en sí, no. Tengo un acuario con peces tropicales de todos colores – rojos, negros amarillos. Hay grandes y pequeños. Son tranquilos. Los puedo mirar por horas.

3 – Pilar, tú tienes una cabra ¿no es así?
– Sí, así es – se llama Trudi. Es blanca y pequeña. Me encanta jugar con ella porque es una cabrita muy traviesa.

4 – Y Guillermo. ¡Tú qué tienes?
– En mi casa tenemos pájaros en jaulas. Canarios amarillos y verdes que cantan y trillan sin cesar. Son lindos y pequeños.

5 – Aquí soy yo, Anita, con mi perrita. Se llama Bela. Es pequeña y de dos colores, blanco y negro. Es adorable y la quiero mucho.

6 – Roberto, tienes un caballito galés. ¿Cierto?
– Si, es castaño con una cola larga. Es manso y contento y bastante bajo.

7 – Aquí estoy yo, Leonardo, con una culebra grande y peligrosa. Es amarilla con manchas verdes. ¡Cuidado!

8 – ¿Y tú Marta?
– En mi casa no hay animales porque a mis padres no les gustan. A mí sí, y me gustaría tener un gato gris con rayas blancas, ni grande ni pequeño – más bien mediano, y muy cariñoso.

---

animal	color	tamaño	característica

In these two examples, we can differentiate 'listening to learn (the foreign language)' and 'learning to listen (in the foreign language)'. One sort of listening is not better than the other. They serve different purposes so we need both sorts of texts.

Authentic material

I defined this earlier as material produced for language users rather than language learners. It covers a whole range of subject matter from family discussions to heated political debates, from the news to announcements in shops and railway stations. Some of it is very difficult for the foreign language learner because it is structurally complex and culturally specific. Advanced level learners have to be able to cope with it. Subject matter of interest is more likely to motivate learners to rise to the challenge of working with such texts. Simplification of recorded material is impossible so listeners will benefit from preparatory work, opportunities to control the tape for themselves and graded tasks.

Learners need to be exposed to a range of different text types – realistic pedagogic material and, for some, authentic material. A key question we must ask ourselves is whether a particular piece of recorded material will be **effective** in helping our learners to get better. The way learners might progress from something strictly controlled to a more open-ended sort of spoken text might be like this:

| **1** | Hearing and identifying new language patterns in simple statements or through graded question and answer work. This presentation might be supported by visuals and may very well be carried out by the teacher rather than through recorded material. |

| **2** | Understanding the new language item in combination with known language in a more realistic but still controlled setting – for example a dialogue or an interview. |

| **3** | Understanding the new language item in a more open-ended context where known language is recycled from the past and unknown language appears and where speakers are speaking at a rate approaching native speaker speed. The focus at this stage is on what is being said, on the message, not on the language structures being used. Learners are coping with language which is beyond what they might produce in speech themselves. |

Grading tasks

The purpose of setting tasks to accompany a piece of listening is to guide learners through. It is not to catch them out or find out what they do not know. The tasks we set should therefore **support** listening. They do this by directing the learner's attention to the key information required from the text and by preparing the way for what is to be heard. Here is a Spanish girl describing herself. Before hearing the recording, learners look at the task.

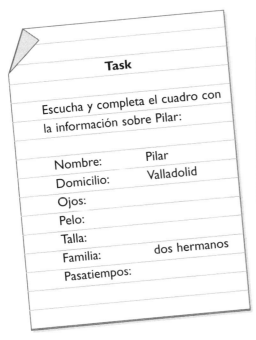

Task

Escucha y completa el cuadro con la información sobre Pilar:

Nombre: Pilar
Domicilio: Valladolid
Ojos:
Pelo:
Talla:
Familia: dos hermanos
Pasatiempos:

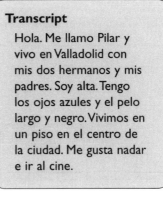

Transcript

Hola. Me llamo Pilar y vivo en Valladolid con mis dos hermanos y mis padres. Soy alta. Tengo los ojos azules y el pelo largo y negro. Vivimos en un piso en el centro de la ciudad. Me gusta nadar e ir al cine.

The task informs listeners what the text is about; it directs their attention to the specific information required, i.e. it shows them what to listen out for; it is quickly completed. An alternative task could have a multiple-choice format:

Task	
Escucha y escoge la respuesta adecuada:	
1 Pilar es alta.	3 Tiene el pelo negro y corto.
Pilar es baja.	Tiene el pelo negro y largo.
2 Tiene los ojos azules.	4 Le gusta nadar.
Tiene los ojos verdes.	Le gusta jugar al tennis.

This task provides more information from the text itself and also limits possible choices; it would be much quicker to complete (a tick). Its disadvantages are that, even with the choice limited to one out of two, there is a lot more to read (possibly a disadvantage for some learners) and the task is less 'life-like'. However, the personal information form in the first example could be completed as a **reading and writing task** afterwards.

I like listening tasks that require the completion of a grid. Grids allow us to provide all the support mentioned above but they have a useful flexibility about them. Here is an example taken from the Exemplification of Standards (1996) – a document produced to help teachers assign a National Curriculum level to pupils' work. Pupils listen to the tape and record in the grid which school subjects the five French pupils like and dislike.

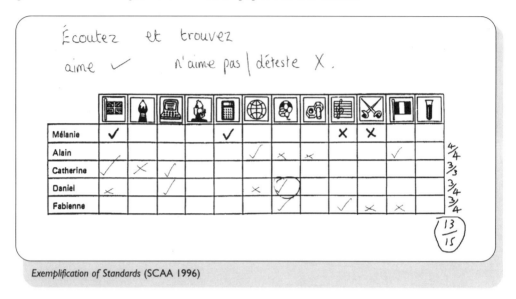

Exemplification of Standards (SCAA 1996)

The supportive elements in the grid are these:

- the column headings indicate the nature of the information required (these school subjects and no others);
- the proper names are provided so that learners know exactly how many speakers there are;
- an example is completed to show exactly what needs to be done and how;
- the key phrases (*aime*; *n'aime pas*) are provided as prompts;
- answers are recorded in the form of ticks and crosses which are quickly completed and therefore appropriate to the fleeting nature of speech.

The only difficulty I can see here is the number of subjects to be scanned before an answer can be recorded.

There are other advantages to working with grids which will become apparent in the next section.

Integrating listening into the other skill areas

We talk about the four skills as discrete items for planning and assessment purposes but in real-life, we mix and combine the skills all the time. As I pointed out in Chapter 1, listening and speaking are inseparable in the young first language learner. Throughout our daily lives we read and make comments; we listen and write.

In classroom foreign language learning, the skills need to be integrated in the same way. The language learning we do through listening needs to be connected with the language learning we do through speaking, reading or writing. If learners are to develop the automatic word recognition essential to the comprehension process, then they need to keep what they know in constant circulation. Clearly focused oral work – and some writing too – might precede a listening activity, and post-listening activities can consolidate what has been heard through reading and writing, which are more self-paced and reflective activities. In the last activity on page 26, for example, oral revision of school subjects will precede the listening activity. Answers can be checked in a variety of graded ways depending on the speaking skills of the learners. For example, **the teacher** could ask questions which require only the name of the school subject as an answer:

> – Qu'est-ce qu'Alain aime? Qu'est-ce qu'il n'aime pas?

Individual learners could **provide oral statements**, i.e. they **generate** their own sentences from the data:

> – Catherine aime l'anglais. Elle n'aime pas les sciences.
>   Or
> – Catherine aime l'anglais mais elle n'aime pas les sciences.

Individual learners could **ask each other questions**, i.e. they **generate** questions based on the data:

> – Est-ce que Daniel aime la géographie?
> – Qu'est-ce que Daniel aime?

This sort of grading allows learners to work at different levels and there is no reason why the teacher should not use a variety of techniques for completing the grid.

Once the accuracy of answers has been checked and recorded, then one or several of the activities below based on the data collected in the grid might follow on effectively:

- **learners** work in **pairs** to **ask each other** questions based on the data in the grid;
- learners **read** a series of statements and indicate whether they are true or false – they correct what is false;
- learners answer questions in **writing**;
- learners **create** some written statements about the interests of the speakers which include the use of **plural** verbs (*Catherine et Daniel* **aiment** *l'informatique*) or conjunctions (*Fabienne aime le sport et la musique* **mais** *il n'aime pas le français*);
- learners **talk** and **write about** their **own interests**.

Within this follow-up work, we can see that there are possibilities not only for work directed by the teacher from the front, but also for work with some element of control from the front – individual learners asking the whole class questions (a sort of half-way house on the road to pairwork) and also for work carried out in pairs for later correction by the teacher or by the class as a whole.

We can also see that some activities are more difficult than others. Answering a true/false question is much less demanding linguistically than **generating** an oral or written statement from the data provided. The former is a receptive activity, the latter a productive one. In this way teachers can provide a range of tasks suited to the level of competence of the learners in any specific group.

Learner strategies

In the 1990s, interest grew in the way learners used particular strategies to help them with foreign language learning. Rost (2002:154) tells us that 'expert performance in any behaviour involves planning and selection of appropriate strategies' so all learners need to develop and use a range of strategies.

Strategies, according to the research literature, can be described as: tactics or plans, behaviours and thoughts, techniques or approaches; but the defining element is that the action is **deliberate** and **consciously selected** on the part of the individual to support understanding and help learning. In the literature, writers refer to 'learn**ing** strategies' and 'learn**er** strategies', using the two terms synonymously. Macaro (2001: 20) argues the case for the term 'learn**er** strategies' because, for him, it captures effectively the emphasis he wants to put on the learner as 'active participant' in the learning process. I am persuaded by this approach because the emphasis is very much on developing learner confidence and independence. Learn**ing** strategies are then one type of strategy used by individuals.

Researchers categorise strategies in different ways and the boundaries overlap somewhat. In terms of developing (one-way) listening skills, we should be particularly interested in:

- listening strategies,
- memorisation strategies,
- metacognitive (or monitoring) strategies.

Harris (in Harris and Snow 2004) lists **listening strategies** in helpfully learner-friendly terms, as shown opposite.

The 'before listening' strategies tie in well with the pre-listening activities we outlined on page 17 – the ones which provided learners with a framework for listening. In order to develop strategy use, teachers should encourage learners to take the lead in preparation for listening by gradually handing over responsibility for thinking and planning ahead. Harris's checklist is very useful for this. Thinking ahead is a metacognitive strategy – see page 30.

Checklist of listening strategies

Before listening	✓
I check that I understand the task I have to do	
I look carefully at the title and any pictures to see if I can guess what it will be about	
I try to remember as many words as I can to do with this topic	
I think about what is likely to be said in this situation and predict the words I am likely to hear	

While listening	✓
I work out if it is a conversation, an advert, a news bulletin, etc	
I pay attention to the tone of voice and any background noises for clues	
I use other clues like key words to identify the rough gist	
I use my common sense to make sensible guesses	
I try to see if any words are like words in English	
I don't panic when there is something I don't understand, but I carry on listening	
I listen out for the names of people or places	
I try to hold the difficult sounds in my head and say them over and over again	
I try to break down the stream of sounds into individual words and write them down to see if they are like words I recognise	
I don't give up and just make wild guesses	
I listen out for grammar clues like tenses, pronouns	

After listening	✓
I check back to see if my first guesses were right and made sense or I need to think again	
I think about why some of the strategies I used did not work and which could help me more next time	

© CILT, the National Centre for Languages 2004

Memorisation strategies are essential because the more words and phrases a learner can commit to memory for later rapid retrieval, the less mental processing time will be required for bottom-up word level processing. More processing time can be then be spent on working at global meaning. Macaro (2001: 119) and Grenfell and Harris (1999: 130) list, again in helpful learner-friendly language, the following strategies for committing language to memory:

- practise saying new words out loud at home;
- learn by a system that suits you (e.g. look, hide, say, write, check);
- make mental associations or visual links;
- learn sets of words;
- link new words to known words;
- turn language into songs, rhymes, raps or mnemonics;
- act out language at home;
- record on a tape;
- repeat words to yourself when you hear them in class;
- test each other;
- do silent practice, thinking in your head;
- make a note of new words.

See also Snow (in Harris and Snow 2004) for further ideas.

Metacognitive strategies are concerned with monitoring and evaluating learning. According to O'Malley and Chamot (1990) and Bacon (1992) both quoted in Macaro (2001: 73 and 101), successful language learners monitor and evaluate their learning in the following sorts of ways. They:

- preview the task to be completed and think about the kind of answer needed;
- focus their attention on the tasks, concentrate and try to avoid distractions;
- decide in advance to focus on specific aspects of the text;
- have a plan for listening (e.g. listening out for key words, time indicators, negatives, comparisons or qualifiers like 'a lot', 'a few', 'often');
- understand how they best learn;
- monitor their understanding and progress.

The good news about strategies is that they can be taught. Good strategy instruction can be linked to the sorts of discussions under the heading 'Talking to learners about the listening process on pages 14–17 and has the following characteristics:

- exploratory discussion between teacher and learners;
- explanation and modelling by teacher;
- sharing of strategies amongst learners;
- practise of a range of strategies, together with monitoring of effectiveness by learners;
- integration into the scheme of work over an extended period of time (not short one-off sessions);
- application to classroom work (not isolated examples).

For ideas on integrating listening strategies into the scheme of work, see Harris (Harris and Snow 2004: 39–42). For ideas on 'the cycle of strategy instruction in action' and details on consciousness raising, modelling, practice and monitoring, see Grenfell and Harris (1999) Chapters 4 and 5. These authors also report on some interesting case studies of strategy instruction in foreign language learning based in English secondary schools.

3　Texts and tasks

In this chapter, the focus will be listening to understand information rather than listening to learn the structures of the language. We shall need descriptions, narrations, discussions, reports, messages, transactional and interactional dialogues, presentations of varying lengths. Suitable texts may well be beyond the productive linguistic competence of the listeners. They will contain much familiar language, some of it recycled from earlier units in the coursebook, and possibly some unfamiliar or new language whose meaning may be derived from context. For most learners, the speed of delivery will increasingly move towards that of the native speaker as they progress through the course, for coping with 'natural' language is something we learn to do over time. We noted in Chapter 2 that learners need to work with such material in each module or unit of work so that there is progression through a module and through the course as a whole.

GRADING THE DIFFICULTY OF LISTENING ACTIVITIES

In order to grade our material over a period of time, we need to identify the features of recorded spoken texts that will influence the degree of difficulty experienced by learners. In the table below, I have pulled together the different aspects of recorded spoken language which need to be taken into account, together with the increasing demands of the task.

Each column represents the sorts of issues that have to be taken into consideration in assessing the difficulty of any listening activity. Let us now look in further detail at each.

Source

We have already discussed the merits of pedagogic and authentic texts in the previous chapter. We need to recall here that in materials recorded for **users** of the language, we have **no control** over any of the aspects under consideration under 'speaker' and 'content', whereas in pedagogic texts coursebook writers and examination boards can exercise greater or lesser control over any aspect. Thus, in a discussion between two or three people about a fairly complex issue, where speakers would normally speak very quickly and cut each other off in order to put their opinion across, we control the amount of interjecting and the speed of delivery. This is what currently happens in GCSE Listening texts at Higher Level.

SOURCE	SPEAKER(S)	CONTENT	TASK
pedagogic	one or more	**medium:** vocabulary structural range sentence complexity	recognise
	monologue dialogue conversation discussion		note facts: gist detail
	all male voices all female voices		note opinions
authentic	formality informality factual/abstract colloqiality	**message:** familiar content new factual/abstract	demands on memory
	accent	explicitly stated implicitly – to be inferred	interpret
	speed of delivery	sequentially organised	infer

Speakers

In listening to recorded material, following two or more speakers is more difficult than following one unless the change of speaker is clearly marked by, for example, distinctive turn-taking (waiter and customer in restaurant) or by different tones of voice. It is much harder to differentiate between two or three female voices than a mixture of male and female voices. Over and above the number of speakers, we need to consider the degree of formality/informality of the language. Informal conversations are marked by unfinished sentences, swallowed words, hesitations and a stop-start delivery because they are spontaneous, that is, not planned and thought out. This may be confusing. However, they are also marked by repetition and rewordings which can be very useful to learners. Spoken language which is planned, for example, like radio news bulletins, tends to have a more even delivery and clearer enunciation but the very fact that it is planned means there will be little redundancy and it can be delivered at a very rapid rate. The speaker does not need time to think. This is why on the television news today listeners are frequently given a synopsis of what will be reported before the full report and are then told at the end what they have been listening to.

Content

The points noted in this column are self-explanatory. Factual information is easier to understand than abstract, and explicitly given information is easier to understand than that which has to be inferred. Making inferences entails listening and understanding the information, holding on to what has been understood and taking it a step further, or it may entail 'making the missing links'.

Tasks

In this column, there is a clear sense of grading from top to bottom. Tasks which involve recognition (ticking the items on someone's shopping list from a more general list provided) are much less demanding than those which make cognitive demands such as interpreting. However, as we said in the previous chapter, grading of tasks is not just concerned with the demands of the task itself, but also with the amount of support provided. Supplying pictorial or textual support with a task makes the job that much easier.

MIXING AND MATCHING TEXTS AND TASKS

In grading our listening, we can mix and match texts and tasks. If we want learners to tackle a fairly demanding listening text, then we can set an undemanding task which provides plenty of support. If the text is simple, we can set a more demanding task.

Here is an idea for using the same simple task with two different texts where the second text is more difficult than the first. The task is to write a shopping list.

Text 1 might consist of one person telling another what to buy; a clearly enunciated monologue where mother tells son, for example, what she needs from the supermarket. Listeners play the role of the son and write down, in the order spoken, the items required. This would be fairly realistic as we speak more slowly when someone is writing down what we say.

Text 2 might consist of two people discussing what dishes to prepare for a supper-party and what ingredients they need to buy. This would involve a dialogue, possibly with some interjecting and some agreement and disagreement about who likes what, about what ingredients were already in store, etc.

Examples are provided later in the chapter of how to vary the task but keep the text the same in order to cater for different levels of linguistic competence.

The overall difficulty of any listening activity is a function of the interplay between text and task. We do not simultaneously increase the difficulty of text and task. We shall look at this in more detail later in the chapter, but it might be useful at this stage to identify the easiest and the most difficult sort of oral text:

The easiest	The most difficult
• one speaker	• several speakers interacting
• visual support (video, pictures)	• audio only
• repetition of the message	• rapid change of speaker
• time to get used to the speaker's voice	• fast, unclear speech
• clearly enunciated speech	• unfamiliar context
• familiar context	• abstract content
• little to remember	• memory demands
• clear sequence of events	• inferences to be made
• no inferences to be made	

Of course, there is one essential variable in all this that I have not yet taken into account: **the listener**. Texts and tasks are only difficult in relation to the individual who is listening. Listeners have different motivations, bring different experiences and expectations to the classroom. They have different background knowledge to draw on. All these have a part to play in grading the listening. Brown and Yule, quoted in Anderson and Lynch (1988), make a useful analogy which helps to 'capture the complexity' of grading:

> *Think of the control panel in a recording studio. The recording engineers have in front of them a set of slide controls which they can adjust to any point between zero and maximum. Each of the slides contributes to the desired blend of voices, instruments, pre-recorded background noises and so on. For Brown and Yule, there are four main slide controls. Each of these can be set at any point, independently of the precise setting of the other slides, as in the diagram below:*

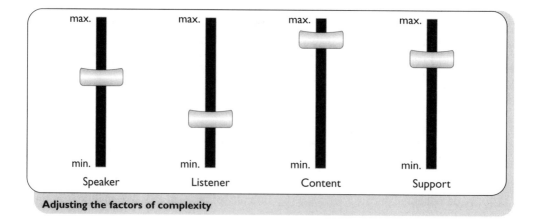

Adjusting the factors of complexity

We have to bear in mind that each of these slide controls represents a combination of factors. For example, in deciding the level at which you should set the 'speaker' control you have to consider the relevant component factors: how many speakers are actively involved in the text, the speed at which some of them (those participants whose ideas and comments you want the learners to focus on) talk to each other, and the likely familiarity of their accents for your students.'

DIFFERENTIATING THE TASKS

The principles underlying the following tasks make them suitable for any level of text and any level of learner. The details will, of course, vary. Some suggestions are:

TASKS	EXAMPLES
listen and put in chronological order according to the tape	• a set of pictures • a number of items • a sequence of events • the news headlines
listen and select	• people being described on a photo • a suitable job from the Jobs page • five key points from a list of ten to summarise the text
listen and follow	• a map, a street plan • instructions • colours for clothes, hair, eyes • a written text to find factual differences
listen and complete	• forms, diaries, grids, graphs, barcharts • missing details on a picture • who?, what?, when?, how?, grids
listen and write	• answers to questions • fill gaps • notes
listen and speak	• paraphrase for non-language speaker • translate • take a role in a dialogue
listen and make a decision	• based on the weather forecast • about a holiday destination • who to support politically
listen and infer	• moods • roles and relationships • attitudes and opinions

From top to bottom of the list, the tasks become increasingly demanding. Moreover, the amount of support, visual or verbal, offered by the task decreases as we move down the list, making the task harder. Let us look at a few examples more concretely to see how the same sort of task might be used with a wide range of learners of different ages and abilities:

Listen and put in order

For the Year 7 child with special needs, this might entail putting a series of pictures (fruit, groceries, rooms in a house) in order as they are heard on the tape. This could be performed by arranging cut-out pictures on the desk or by numbering the items on a worksheet. For the AS level learner, it might entail putting the news headlines in order from a radio recording. In the first example, the support provided by the task is pictorial in nature; in the second, it is textual but in both cases it serves the same purpose. It provides a framework and sets the parameters for listening before the recording is heard and it provides a stimulus for (oral) preparatory work.

Here are some news headlines which appeared while I was writing this book:

"Patrick Vieira n'ira pas au Réal Madrid!"

"Avant même le début des Jeux Olympiques, deux athlètes grecs risquent la suspension."

"L'Imam chiite Moqtada al-Sadr aurait été blessé pendant la bataille de Nadjaf."

"L'économie française est assurée d'enregistrer au minimum 2,2% de croissance en 2004."

Learners might be invited to suggest an order of presentation before they hear the recording and to provide a simple explanation. For example:

La guerre en Iraq est plus importante que le football parce que …

At this level, the pre-listening work may well include the introduction of key vocabulary and/or the input of cultural information.

Listen and follow

Learners in the early stages of foreign language learning might be asked to follow, for example:

- a street plan: how to get to the cinema;
- a set of instructions: for putting furniture in a bedroom;
- details for colouring in: faces, clothes.

At the more advanced end of the range, learners might follow a witness's written statement and listen out for inconsistencies in the recorded follow-up interview.

Listen and write

Writing might consist of single words, such as a checklist for packing a suitcase for the holidays, or it might consist of making notes, unsupported, on the key points made by a speaker, for example on pollution.

Listen and make a decision

Tasks here might be as simple as listening to the weather forecast and deciding whether to go for a picnic or to paint your bedroom, or as complex as deciding who to vote for after hearing their policies.

Listen and infer

As we have already said, this involves understanding what is not explicitly stated. It might involve weighing up roles and relationships between individuals, or commenting on someone's personality from the details they provide of their pastimes or someone's attitude from a dialogue (for example, male asks female out – or vice versa, and female – or male – makes a number of excuses why she/he cannot make the cinema, the restaurant, the drive to the coast).

In the table of suggested listening tasks on page 35 it is clear to see that as we move down the list, the support mechanism inherent in the nature of the tasks at the top of the list is gradually removed. As we get to the bottom of the list, not only does the task itself become linguistically and cognitively more demanding, but the visual and/or verbal support provided by the task disappears.

WORKING AT DIFFERENT LEVELS AND BEING MORE ADVENTUROUS

Listening can also take place as part of a carousel of activities or as part of collaborative group and class work. These sorts of arrangements take time to plan and organise, so they probably do not occur frequently. They need to have a long shelf life, that is, we need to be able to use them more than once or twice so that they are worth the time and effort invested.

In a carousel arrangement, listening is just one of a series of activities to be completed during the lesson. A listening centre with headphones is desirable so that the listening group can hear the recording clearly without disturbing others and, more importantly, can control the number of pauses and replays according to needs. (AS and A level candidates have individual control of recorded material in the examination so that they can replay at will as many times as required). Other activities might involve reading a text, finding information from a website or oral work with the teacher/language assistant. Learners work their way through some or all of the activities as directed by the teacher or according to choice. They can either work as individuals or collaboratively.

In a jigsaw arrangement, learners work collaboratively within a group. They collect information from a variety of sources, spoken and written, which they then feedback in the foreign language to other groups in the class. The total information collected completes a story or offers different perspectives on a theme.

The benefits of working in these ways are:

- flexibility of grouping: friendship, level of proficiency;
- choice of activity: some prefer to read, others to listen;
- opportunities to integrate work in different skill areas;
- responsibility and independence of learners: they need to be organised and to report back to others;
- release for the teacher who is able to circulate and monitor or work with groups;
- mixed skill working.

4 Using TV and other resources

SUPPLEMENTING RECORDINGS WHICH ACCOMPANY COURSEBOOKS

There are many reasons for using recorded television programmes regularly in our teaching. They provide variety, of course, and they supplement the range of material at our disposal in planning the development of listening skills over a period of time. The BBC and Channel 4 produce a wealth of regularly updated programmes targeted at particular learners (adults and school learners from primary to advanced level). The material is often closely linked to the sorts of topics that schools must cover for the National Curriculum and, linguistically, it presents in action some of the vocabulary and structures specified in examination syllabuses. Furthermore, it often comes with transcripts and ideas for exploitation! Details of programmes can be found for the BBC at **www.bbc.co.uk/languages** and for Channel 4 at **www.channel4.com/learning/main/secondary/modlang.htm**.

CONTEXTUALISING THE LANGUAGE

In this short chapter we cannot go into great detail about the use of the television in the classroom, but we can review its advantages in the light of the double decontextualisation of audio recordings which we identified in Chapter 2. The visual aspects of the television can supply many of the missing contextual features of audio recordings by:

* providing a cultural setting for the speakers and the action;
* providing paralinguistic features such as facial expressions, gestures, body language.

Television brings into the classroom the world of the foreign language in a way no other medium can. Other than going to the country itself, which many of our learners may never do, there is no better way of seeing its geography, history and social life. In addition to this cultural backdrop, we can also see the speakers and learn to use what we see to help understanding of what is being said – are the speakers smiling, making angry gestures, shrugging their shoulders, indicating something with their hands? Moreover, television material, because it is often recorded on location, can provide us with a range of regional accents.

MAKING MEANING CLEARER

Perhaps the most compelling reason for using television as part of developing listening is that what learners see can help them to understand what they hear. A good guiding principle in judging the pedagogic worth of video material is the extent to which the sound and the visual complement each other, that is the extent to which the pictures make the meaning of the language clear (or clearer). Learners have to be taught to 'read' the picture, but we can do this by capitalising on one of the technological advantages of the medium, by turning down the sound, which also allows us to do some useful oral work. If a commentary is telling us about the old part of a city, or about what you can buy in particular shops, then the pictures should be focused on the old buildings and the merchandise rather than on the face of the speaker. 'Talking heads', whether one or two, are not necessarily any improvement on audio recordings except, of course, that any change of speaker is obvious. Pedagogic television usually gets the balance right by interspersing action scenes with brief interviews between a presenter and local people, and this is where learners benefit from seeing the paralinguistic features mentioned above and from hearing a range of registers and possibly some regional accents.

ACTIVITIES

The appeal of the television for some learners may lie in its links with the outside world but we need to impress upon them that viewing in the classroom is not like watching the television at home where it is often on as a backdrop to other activities without receiving any concentrated attention.

Television material needs to be integrated into normal classroom work in the same way as audio material. Pre- and post-viewing activities will prepare learners for what they are to see and consolidate what they have understood. All the issues raised earlier about the need for activities to be appropriate to the fleeting nature of speech are equally applicable to activities designed to accompany viewing, for if learners' heads are lowered to write lengthy answers they cannot be looking at the screen.

Short snippets of television material go a long way. Five minutes is plenty if learners are to view several times. Pedagogic material is often designed so that each programme can be divided into shorter sections.

OTHER RESOURCES FOR KEY STAGES 3 AND 4

The BBC Languages website (**www.bbc.co.uk/languages**) offers excellent listening opportunities at different levels. The BBC Bitesize programmes provide audio texts at Foundation and Higher level for learners preparing for GCSE examinations in French, German and Spanish. These can be used in Revise or Test mode and there is a good range of appropriate topics.

From the BBC Languages Home Page learners can access the 'Better at listening' pages, by clicking on the 'Become a better listener' hotlink in the 'Help with learning languages' box. These contain snippets from real-life situations in French, German, Italian and Spanish. The short recordings involve native speakers speaking at normal speed. Activities are provided to help listeners assess their skills and strategies for improving are suggested.

OTHER RESOURCES FOR ADVANCED LEARNERS

Le Mensuel (French) and *El Mensual* (Spanish), accessed from the BBC languages website are monthly intermediate audio magazines for AS and A level students. The topical and archived news reports are matched to current advanced level syllabus topics. Furthermore, the audio texts can be read and printed out and there is an on-line dictionary. Songs from current pop stars, aural texts on cultural themes and video clips also feature. For learners of German, there are video clips in *Deutsch Plus*.

From the same BBC website, learners can listen to the BBC World News in Spanish (see **http://news.bbc.co.uk/hi/spanish/news**).

CILT Information sheets, which can be downloaded from the CILT website (**www.cilt.org.uk/infos**) include many helpful suggestions for supplementary materials for developing listening. Information sheet 32 (French), 48 (German), 49 (Spanish) list the relevant software available in the CILT library. Information sheets 65 (French), 66 (German) and 68 (Spanish) list A level teaching materials. All of these contain resources for listening.

Some films on DVD offer a choice of languages, so snippets from a familiar film with foreign language sound track could provide good exposure to native speakers speaking at normal speed, as well as opportunities for oral description and narration.

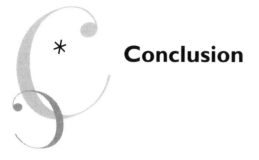

Conclusion

Listening in a foreign language is not easy. We must not underestimate the difficulties facing learners. They need help to improve and progress. The demands made by public examinations are high but there is consistency across institutions about what constitutes progress in the development of listening skills in communicative contexts.

The Council of Europe *Common European Framework of Reference for Languages* (**www.coe.int/T/E/Cultural_Co-operation/education/Languages/Language_policy**) provides a cross-European basis for the mutual recognition of language qualifications to facilitate educational and occupational mobility. The Framework, which covers the four language skills, will be used increasingly in the design of national curricula and assessment systems. Progression in listening from beginner to mastery is defined in terms of the following features of spoken text:

- length of text;
- speed of delivery;
- clarity of expression;
- complexity of sentence structure;
- range of text type;
- familiarity of content;
- complexity of subject matter;
- cultural embeddedness.

These features are clearly recognisable as strands running through the level descriptions of Attainment Target 1 (Listening and Responding) in the English National Curriculum for Modern Foreign Languages (DfES 1999) and they are evident in the progression from GCSE Foundation and Higher to AS and A2 examination texts.

As part of the National Languages Strategy, the Department for Education and Skills is mapping onto the Common European Framework its own 'Languages Ladder' (see **www.dfes.gov.uk/languages/languagesladder.cfm**). The Languages Ladder relates national assessment systems to the six levels of the European Framework. Self-assessment grids with 'can do' statements for each level are available and, in the Appendix, I show a comparison between the national assessment levels and those of the European Framework for the skill of listening. For school learners, relating their level of proficiency to a wider framework which applies to everyone (not just learners in school but adults across Europe) could be very motivating.

This consistency in expectations helps with long-term planning and with differentiating for different levels of proficiency. We can plan the development of listening skills over a period of time so that we provide learners with a range of text types at a level of difficulty appropriate to their linguistic competence. Learners need to listen to more than the recorded material which accompanies their coursebook and new technologies, like CD-ROMs, DVDs and Web-based material, have made available good quality recordings which can be used by individuals as required.

Finally a word about the use of tapescripts. If we allow listeners to follow a tapescript whilst the tape is playing, then the activity becomes a reading activity. Having access to the printed word takes away the ephemeral nature of the spoken word, it is true; but the fleeting nature of spoken language is precisely what learners have to learn to cope with. If they become dependent on seeing the words rather than learning to cope with only hearing them, then we are not developing listening skills and we are not doing them a service at all. This is equally true when the teacher repeats what the tape has said. Learners are dependent on one voice, one accent, one speed of delivery. There are, however, occasions when it is useful to have a tapescript. For example, for pronunciation practice. As has been mentioned earlier, words are at times pronounced quite differently in sentences compared to when they are pronounced in isolation. Spoken informal language is spoken quite differently from its written form. Words are 'eaten up' or disappear altogether; stress and intonation are not shown in the written form. These would seem to be appropriate occasions for the use of a tapescript.

National Qualifications and the Common European Framework of Reference for Languages

LISTENING

National qualifications levels	Grade descriptions	Common European Framework levels	Level descriptions
National Curriculum for Modern Foreign Languages: Level 3	Understand short passages (e.g. instructions, messages, dialogues) made up of familiar language spoken at near normal speed without interference with repetition if needed. Identify and note main points and personal responses.	Breakthrough A1	Recognise familiar words and very basic phrases concerning myself, my family and immediate concrete surroundings when people speak slowly and clearly.
GCSE Foundation Grade F	Identify main points and extract some details from simple language spoken clearly at near normal speed.	Waystage A2	Understand phrases and the highest frequency vocabulary related to areas of most immediate personal relevance (e.g. personal and family information, shopping, local area, employment). Catch the main point in short clear simple messages and announcements.
GCSE Higher Grade C	Identify and note main points and extract details and points of view from language spoken at normal speed covering a variety of topics that include familiar language in unfamiliar contexts.	Threshold B1	Understand the main points of clear standard speech on familiar matters regularly encountered in work, school, leisure. Understand the main point of many radio or TV programmes on current affairs or topics of personal or professional interest when the delivery is relatively slow and clear.
AS/A level Grade A	Understand a wide range of complex language in a variety of registers. Understand grammatical markers like tense and mood; awareness of structure, style and register. Understand detail and make inferences.	Vantage B2	Understand extended speech and lectures and follow even complex lines of argument, provided the topic is reasonably familiar. Understand most TV news and current affairs programmes and the majority of films in standard dialect.
		Operational proficiency C1	Understand extended speech even when it is not clearly structured and when relationships are only implied and not signalled explicitly. Understand television programmes and films without too much effort.
		Mastery C2	Understand any kind of spoken language, whether live or broadcast, even when delivered at fast native speed; time may be needed to become familiar with the accent.

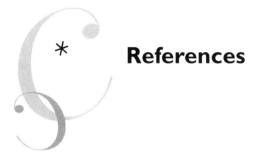

References

Alonso de Sudea, I. and Sookias, H. (1998) *Español a la vista, Guía del profesor*. Oxford University Press.

Anderson, A. and Lynch, T. (1988) *Listening*. Oxford University Press.

Bourdais, D., Finnie, S. and Gordon, A. L. (1998) *Equipe 1, Livre du professeur*. Oxford University Press.

Council of Europe (2001) *Common European Framework of Reference for Languages: Learning, teaching, assessment*. Cambridge University Press.

Department for Education and Employment (2001): *The Key Stage 3 National Strategy Framework for teaching English: Years 7, 8, 9*. HMSO.

Department for Education and Employment/Qualifications and Curriculum Authority (1999) *Modern Foreign Languages. The National Curriculum for England*. HMSO.

Department for Education and Skills (2003) *Speaking, listening and learning: Working with children in Key Stages 1 and 2. Teaching objectives and classroom activities*. HMSO.

Department for Education and Skills (2003): *The Key Stage 3 National Strategy Framework for teaching Modern Foreign Languages: Years 7, 8 and 9*, DfES.

Donaldson, M. (1978) *Children's minds*. Fontana Press.

Grabe, W. and Stoller, L. (2002) *Teaching and Researching Reading*. Pearson Education Ltd.

Grenfell, M. and Harris, V. (1999) *Modern Languages and learning strategies in theory and practice*. Routledge.

Harris, V. and Snow, D. (2004) *Classic Pathfinder 4: Doing it for themselves: Focus on learning strategies and vocabulary building*. CILT, the National Centre for Languages.

Harrison, C. (1996) *The teaching of reading. What teachers need to know*. UK Reading Association (UKRA).

Hawkins, E. (1987) *Awareness of language: An introduction*. Cambridge University Press.

Macaro, E. (2001) *Learning strategies in foreign and second language classrooms*. Continuum.

Macaro, E. (2003) *Teaching and learning a second language*. Continuum.

Rost, M. (2002) *Teaching and researching: Listening*. Longman.

School Curriculum and Assessment Authority (1996) *Exemplification of Standards*. SCAA.

Swarbrick, A. (1998) *Pathfinder 36: More reading for pleasure*. CILT.

Turner, K. (2002) *Developing listening skills*. In: Swarbrick, A. (ed) *Aspects of teaching Modern Foreign Languages: Perspectives on practice*. RoutledgeFalmer.

FURTHER READING

Fawkes, S. (1998) *Switched on? Video resources in modern language settings*. Multilingual Matters.

Ur, P. (1984) *Teaching listening comprehension*. Cambridge University Press.

White, G. (1998) *Listening*. Oxford University Press.

Part 2

Developing skills for independent reading

IAIN MITCHELL & ANN SWARBRICK

Introduction

The place of reading in the MFL curriculum has long been an issue. With the emergence of a communicative approach, many considered reading to have lost its place to oral and aural activities, to the extent that it began to be highlighted in OFSTED and HMI reports as the 'untaught skill'. Despite the growing recognition of this omission, perceived lack of appropriate materials and pressure of time have often hampered teachers in developing a coherent strategy for reading in the MFL classroom.

This new edition of *Developing skills for independent reading* will discuss ways in which MFL teachers might develop pupils' skills through a planned programme of reading. It will suggest that while it is important for learners to be offered a wide range of texts and to be given opportunities to read them, this in itself will not answer all of the needs of pupils. If pupils are to read successfully in the foreign language, they need to be taught how to do so. This view has been supported in recent years by two significant educational developments: the *National Literacy Strategy*, now firmly embedded in Key Stages 1–3; and, more specifically, the *Framework for teaching Modern Foreign Languages: Years 7, 8 and 9* in England (part of the whole-school *Key Stage 3 National Strategy*).

Secondary teachers who have had no contact with the primary classroom over the past five years may be surprised at the literacy knowledge and skills bases expected of children in Key Stages 1–2. This includes, for example, the *Key Stage 3 Strategy* which builds directly on the *National Literacy Strategy*. It emphasises, in particular, the importance of reading and writing, not just at word and sentence level but, crucially, at 'text level'. Moreover, it also stresses that the skills required for effective reading, particularly of whole and extended texts, are not acquired by a process of osmosis, but need to be specifically taught by the teacher. Thus a key aspect of the *Key Stage 3 Strategy*, that of teacher 'modelling' of a process, has become central in the MFL classroom.

We shall set to our task starting with the assumptions we make about the skills our pupils have when we meet them as beginner linguists (Introduction). We will then discuss the strategies pupils might usefully develop to equip them to function independently when they meet unfamiliar texts (Chapter 1). We will also suggest how teachers might develop these systematically using examples of texts from a variety of sources, including those readily available (but perhaps under-exploited) in coursebooks, and also, increasingly, from authentic documents available on the Internet (Chapter 2). We will finish by focusing on how to develop a policy for independent reading, inside and outside the MFL classroom.

The main changes to this new edition of the Pathfinder aim to reflect the underlying philosophy of these national initiatives, in particular the added importance that is given to 'text level' and 'sentence level' and modelling work. Many of the text examples are new, reflecting the massively increased availability of texts through the medium of the Internet.

WHAT MAY WE ASSUME ABOUT OUR PUPILS?

The prospect of learning a foreign language for many pupils is an exciting one. In the most successful classrooms pupils in their eagerness to speak the language quickly begin to use strategies in the spoken language which they use in their own language. They are not inexperienced communicators; they have a knowledge of many communicative strategies from using their own language. This is also true of their background as readers. They are not learning to read from scratch, they are learning to read in another language. There is an important difference. Most pupils, when they begin learning a language have an implicit knowledge of what it is to read. For example, many understand the significance of genre, they are, in general, able to recognise, say, journalistic register. They have a knowledge of print convention and of layout within different texts: for example, they can differentiate between a children's story and a travel brochure. They have a knowledge of the culture in which they live and this may inform their reading on certain topics. They have an awareness of how a story or argument is structured; that it has a beginning, middle and end. They have a knowledge of punctuation. They will often be able to analyse the text in terms of the techniques being used to encourage the reader to read on, for example, in advertising brochures. They will also now, since the introduction of the *National Literacy Strategy* in primary schools, have more **explicit** awareness of the nature of language, the structure of sentences and will have developed an analytical awareness of how language functions, in particular through its grammar, and how meaning can be developed and refined through a variety of linguistic technical devices.

WHAT SHOULD WE NOT ASSUME ABOUT OUR PUPILS?

No matter how developed both this implicit **and** explicit awareness is in their own language, we cannot assume that it will automatically be transferred to the second language being learnt. Equally, there is a fine line to be drawn between what we feel many pupils **should** know and reality. Though pupils may be able to judge the genre of a text by, for example, considering print convention, there are basic skills which we should not necessarily assume all pupils have, particularly those with learning difficulties. For instance, some pupils may not have a knowledge of alphabetical order, they may not have an awareness that in reading for different purposes the reading process changes: for instance, faced with a page of classified advertisements the skilled reader will scan the page for the information he or she is looking for rather than read every word. Similarly, a pupil may have an awareness of the terminology (of for example grammar and syntax) but may not always be able to apply it effectively to decode meaning in another language. The concept of teacher 'modelling' in whole-class work on a text thus becomes crucial. The teacher demonstrates his or her own thought processes when reading in the foreign language before asking the pupil to do likewise.

In other words, our task is greater than just providing texts for pupils. We need to teach them the reading strategies that will enable them to gain independence as linguists. What these strategies are and how we teach them is the subject of the next chapter.

1 Strategies for reading

STARTING WITH THE PUPILS

What strategies do pupils themselves perceive they use when reading in a foreign language? We gave pupils who had been studying German for a year in a class of mixed attainment the following text and asked them, with a partner, to underline all the words they understood.

Deutschlands Handballer haben die olympische Goldmedaille knapp verpasst. Der Europameister verlor im Finale von Athen gegen Weltmeister Kroatien 24:26 (12:11) und verspielte damit den ersten Olympiasieg einer deutschen Auswahl nach dem Erfolg der DDR-Mannschaft 1980 in Moskau. Bereits 1984 in Los Angeles hatte die Auswahl des Deutschen Handball-Bundes erst im Finale verloren und Silber geholt.

Auch Ronald Rauhe und Tim Wieskötter wurden im Zweier-Kajak ihrer Favoritenstellung gerecht. Das Duo aus Potsdam zog vom Start weg davon und brachte die Führung auch ins Ziel. Silber ging an die Australier Clint Robinson/Nathan Baggaley, Bronze sicherten sich Raman Piatrutschenka/Wadsim Machneuw aus Weißrussland.

Source: **www.olympiade.de**

The results were then pooled and somewhat to their surprise they realised that as a group they understood many of the words in the text. (Though this does beg the question of whether they understood the meaning as a whole as opposed to the individual words.) We asked them to reflect on how they had worked out the meaning of lexical items. Here are some of the strategies they were able to identify:

"I just guessed."

"The text was from an Olympics website."

"I worked it out by seeing what went before and after."

*"I worked out the meaning of the words from
looking them up."*

"I saw it in an advertisement."

Not all pupils were using the same strategies and indeed there were some possibilities that none of them had considered, but this activity highlights the fact that learners do bring some knowledge of how to approach unfamiliar foreign language text. As we mentioned earlier, their experience of reading in their first language has equipped them with some strategies. In other words, they do not come cold to the task of reading. The teacher's role, however, must be to extend the range of strategies for all pupils by explicitly teaching reading strategies.

Let's begin with a few of the comments that our pupils made about the example we gave and consider how to develop some of the strategies they mentioned

Strategy 1

Pupil strategy	Teaching strategy
I worked it out by seeing what went before and after. This strategy refers to familiarity with the linguistic context and with a knowledge of what certain texts look like.	In order to build on this, it may, for example, help pupils to be reminded of such basic information as: • proper nouns will have capital letters; • sentences end with full stops; • punctuation, such as exclamation and question marks, aids comprehension; • many words look similar in both languages; • knowledge of print convention can help understanding (the layout of the page, the particular type of text, e.g. a recipe, a newspaper article).

Strategy 2

Pupil strategy	Teaching strategy
The text was from an Olympics website. This strategy refers to **prediction**. It may then be helpful for pupils to engage in activities that ask them to predict the type of vocabulary they could expect to find in a particular context.	Before seeing the article above, pupils were given the context (*Deutsche Handballer bei den Olympischen Spielen*). This enabled them to predict, with or without the intervention of the teacher, what the article might include details of. For example, names of sports they already know, typical vocabulary of an Olympic webpage (results, teams, medals, countries), typical sentences in sports reports, general knowledge (sports they know the Germans do well in, any information about actual results). A follow-on activity could then be to predict the actual language that might feature in the article.

Pupil strategy	Teaching strategy
I worked out the meaning of the words from looking them up. This strategy underlines the importance of being able to use reference materials such as glossaries and dictionaries.	**Alphabetical order** With some pupils a necessary starting point may be the concept of alphabetical order. Teachers may begin with activities for the pupils such as: • holding word cards and getting into alphabetical order in a line at the front of the class; • sorting words on cards into alphabetical order; • finding the first word in the dictionary beginning with a stated combination of letters; • finding in the dictionary the next or previous word in a sequence. **How the dictionary is organised** While these activities will help with familiarisation with the organisation of a dictionary, activities more specific to finding and checking meaning might include: • matching words with pictures, using the dictionary to check meaning; • choosing a correct definition from a choice of three; • finding the meaning of a word in the shortest possible time; • searching for the next or previous 'header word'. **Finding meaning** Strategies to use here might include: • finding two or three different dictionaries' translation of the same word; • giving three definitions of a word and asking pupils to search for the correct one; • giving a list of compound words and asking pupils to break down each of them, looking up as many different parts as possible in the dictionary, e.g. *Frühstücksfernsehen*; • giving a list of words and asking pupils to check in the dictionary which belong to the same category, e.g. in French *collège, école, écurie, lycée*, and in Spanish *periódico, revista, pluma, libro*. Give pupils a list of words from which they have to look for the 'false friends', e.g. *baskets, cinéma, pull, radio*. **Checking for accuracy** Strategies to use to build the pupil skill checking for accuracy could include: • finding all the feminine nouns on a particular page of the dictionary; • finding the incorrect spelling in a given list of words; • finding the past participles of a given list of verbs; • finding which words in a given list are different forms of the same word, e.g. *Schüler, Schulen, Schülers, Schülern*.

Strategy 4

Pupil strategy	Teaching strategy
I saw it in an advertisement. This refers to the fact that pupils are open to influences outside the classroom and that the teacher is not the only source of language.	It is useful to remind pupils of other areas where they may come across the language in a clear context which will support their comprehension: labels on food and clothes, posters, bilingual public notices, satellite television, radio, foreign language assistant, visitors from the country, British TV advertisements.

Strategy 5

Pupil strategy	Teaching strategy
I just guessed.	While not wanting to encourage wild guessing, guessing within a clear context should be encouraged. The teacher could blank out words in target language headlines and ask pupils to guess the missing word, possibly using the dictionary. We would not wish to suggest that a teacher should spend a whole lesson on any one of these activities but rather that they are viewed as short, quick events which may take place every lesson, once a week or once every other week. What is important is that pupils become accustomed to seeing unfamiliar words and phrases and to using reference materials on a regular basis.

READING THE WHOLE TEXT

Though it is very valuable to encourage pupils to recognise individual lexical items, they must also realise from early on that the whole text is more than the sum of the individual words within it. Pupils need to avoid the view that a text is an agglomeration of individual words each requiring decoding. When we read our mother tongue we consider not just the meaning of individual words, but the whole text in its entirety, be it a quarter page, a half page or a whole book. Encouraging pupils beginning to read in another language to look at the overall structure and message of a text, rather than individual items of information contained in single words, is important. But it is necessary to develop this alongside vocabulary-building activities such as those we have referred to.

Some approaches to whole texts

Jigsaw texts

Rather than presenting pupils with the complete text immediately, they are given a version in which the main sections or paragraphs have been jumbled. Their task is to reorder and compare their finished version with the original. This might be done by cutting and pasting on a computer.

Matching headlines to text

Pupils are presented with a series of short texts from which the titles or headlines have been removed. These are given in a separate list and pupils have to match the headlines and texts.

Weighing up all the evidence

Pupils are presented with a text in which the writer makes both positive and negative statements. They have to decide, on balance, the writer's overall attitude to the subject, e.g. a French visitor compares facilities in a particular town in England and her home town in France. Pupils have to decide, by reading the whole text, which place the writer prefers.

Looking for themes

The teacher provides category headings and the pupils have to find and note all the relevant words in the text, e.g. weather, time, place, movement, feelings, colours.

Typographical layout

To remind pupils how helpful layout can be, they could be given examples of 'raw' texts on the computer where all layout has been removed. The first activity could be to identify which, for example, is the letter, the recipe, the newspaper article, the poster. With the aid of IT this could then be extended into an exercise where pupils have to recreate the original layout.

2 Reading strategies in action: Working with texts

Foreign language coursebooks, especially in the early years of language learning, may provide relatively few extended texts for reading. Where they do occur they are sometimes seen by teachers as an afterthought and pressure to progress through the coursebook may lead to them being omitted. Equally, text work can often be perceived by pupils as only a test. It is important however to move beyond a view of texts merely as providing 'answers to questions' (which can often be on the level of 'what does this word mean?') and see them as central to teaching and learning, and a springboard for work in other skills. The *National Literacy Strategy*, across the curriculum in Key Stages 1–3, and the MFL Framework within the *Key Stage 3 Strategy* in England have begun to change the emphasis, recognising the importance of explicit whole-class work on substantial texts as central to learning, and providing the firm foundations for the development of independent reading. One of the main challenges for MFL teachers is to identify authentic texts that will genuinely engage the learners but that are not so linguistically daunting as to alienate them from the outset. Below we outline some questions to consider when selecting texts to develop independent reading.

WHERE DO TEXTS COME FROM?

The coursebook

Teachers should not constantly feel under pressure to discard material they have to hand and reinvent the wheel. With some fine tuning and a slight shift in the focus and nature of the tasks, it is often possible to breathe fresh life into material that may at first glance appear to have limited potential.

Realia

Brochures, newspapers, letters, posters and handwritten documents by native speakers have always been present in language lessons. To these can now be added electronic contacts from the target language country, e.g. from partner schools in the form of e-mails, faxes and even texting.

The Internet

This has completely transformed the landscape. Texts on any imaginable subject are instantly available in the target language from all countries where the target language is used. This, in itself, can be somewhat overwhelming but acquaintance with some generic types of sites and some specific portals allows the teacher to access appropriate material rapidly. Teachers should, of course, also consider the provenance of text. Is it linguistically accurate, does it display undue bias, etc?

WHAT TEXTS ARE APPROPRIATE FOR WHAT LEARNERS?

It is helpful not to have too blinkered an approach to the concept of levels of difficulty when considering authentic texts. It will not always be necessary for all learners to understand every detail of every text used. Also, using the terminology of the *National Literacy Strategy* and the MFL Framework for England 'word level' is not necessarily shorter/easier and 'text level' is not necessarily harder (or longer) or only appropriate for more able or advanced learners. Example 1 below is an example initially of an 'easy' text question, e.g. *De quoi s'agit-il? Du collège? D'une région de la France? Des moyens du transport?* Equally, Example 5 shows how individual words can offer a challenging task.

HOW IMPORTANT IS READING?

As well as reinforcing key literacy skills, and providing springboards for work in other areas of skill development, authentic texts can help enhance the dimension of cultural awareness. As the Key Stage 3 MFL Framework makes clear (Strand 5), language learning is not just about cracking the linguistic code of a language but also, equally importantly, learning about the societies and individuals who use it, as the following exemplify.

EXAMPLE I FINE TUNING THE COURSEBOOK

Use of a whole text: moving from extensive to intensive work

1 Un parc aquatique dans une ambiance tropicale, avec toboggans vertigineux, piscines à vagues, kamikase, etc.	**4** Authentique ferme du XIXe siècle. Vous êtes invité à découvrir la vie de nos arrière-grands-parents. Reconstitution d'une cuisine-chambre d'autrefois, sa cheminée, son lit, sa vaisselle et son linge.
2 Une découverte de l'espace interactive et originale avec Planétarium, parc Ariane 5, et sa salle d'exposition. Comment lance-t-on une fusée? Comment est fait un satellite?	**5** Une réserve africaine sur 15 hectares. La visite se fait en voiture ou en car. Il y a près de 450 animaux à découvrir.
3 Le plus grand site aéronautique d'Europe. Un tour extérieur en bus, un film documentaire et une vue du hall où sont assemblés les AIRBUS.	**6** La plus grande ville fortifiée d'Europe. Elle compte 52 tours sur 3 km de remparts.

Source: *Métro 3 rouge*. Heinemann (McNab 2002)

In this example the whole text is already presented in user-friendly short sections. Traditionally, learners might only be set question(s) on each section to check comprehension.

An alternative approach is initially to consider **all** the sections together as **one** text, and to adopt a range of approaches that focus on teaching the learners to be better readers, rather than just testing their comprehension.

Exposure to the text

Before using such a text it is well worth recording it on tape, preferably, but not crucially, by a different voice from the teacher's. The first activity can then simply be exposure to the whole text, with pupils listening and following the text, played without a pause. There could then be some open questions: *De quoi s'agit-il? Du collège? Des vacances? Est-ce qu'il y a des mots que vous avez compris?* This activity can remind the learners, right from the start, of the importance of the sound-spelling link as highlighted in the *Key Stage 3 Strategy* MFL Framework.

Quick confidence-boosting tasks

These are aimed at encouraging the learner to scan a text quickly for certain information. A first scan can be quite specific. 'How many times is the word *un* used?' Any 'high re-use' word such as *une/et* would be appropriate. It may appear rather mechanistic, but done with a strict time limit (e.g. 60 seconds), it can involve all, no matter what their ability, and crucially get pupils to quickly scan the whole text.

It is then worth repeating this task, but with more focus on meaning. In the text above pupils could be asked to find as many nouns as possible linked to places for tourists to visit, the main theme of the text. This second scan will take longer than the first but should have a clear time frame (e.g. maximum three minutes).

To develop an awareness of the sound-spelling link pupils could also be challenged to find:

* silent '-s' at the end of French words: e.g. *piscines/assemblés /grand-parents*, etc;
* other silent endings: *vertigineux, animaux, sont, fait, lit*, etc;
* cognates with a different pronunciation in French, e.g. *toboggan, satellite, reconstitution, hectares*;
* words with different spelling but a common final sound (and the odd one out) e.g. *car*; *hectare*; *documentaire*; *remparts*.

Consequently, the pupils have 'looked' at the text three times in quick succession and will have some general familiarity with it before working on more specific comprehension tasks.

Extensive reading: Establishing overall gist

Before becoming involved in detailed comprehension it is worth establishing an awareness of the overall meaning of the text. An effective way of doing this is to provide a 'matching' task with jumbled subheadings for each of the six sections of the text. For example:

Vous aimez voyager?	Vous aimez le sport?	Vous aimez la nature?
L'histoire, c'est intéressant!	Les sciences, c'est super!	

Such a task can be made more challenging by using synonyms. Only having five headings for six sections (one can be used twice) makes the task more challenging (similarly more 'distractor' headings could also be provided).

This can work well as a class activity with teacher 'modelling' either with an OHP or an interactive whiteboard. The teacher might also then ask the pupils to highlight words/clues in each section that substantiate their choice of heading.

An important outcome of this activity is that the pupils now have a brief summary of what the whole text is about.

Intensive reading 1: whole-class modelled work

Rather than then embark on detailed analysis of the whole text, it can be useful to select just one section for detailed class work. For example, this section of the above extract from *Métro* (*Authentique ferme …*) is used with a gap-filling exercise (a task that pupils often find challenging):

Ce bâtiment est un _____ et représente une ferme qui _____ du dix-neuvième siècle. Il y a _____ à voir, surtout la grande _____ où toute la _____ mangeait et dormait. La vie était très _____ à ce temps-là – pas comme _____ !

| animaux | aujourd'hui | beaucoup | château | date | différente |

| famille | jardin | musée | peu | pièce |

| or | aujourd'hui | beaucoup | date | différente |

| famille | musée | pièce |

Source: *Métro 3 rouge*. Heinemann (McNab 2002)

This is an opportunity to **teach** pupils how to approach such a task, rather than to set it as a test. Again, it is ideal for OHP or an interactive whiteboard which can allow pupils physically to drag/write the words into the gaps. It can be 'easier' with only one possible word per gap, or more demanding with an equal number of distractors added. The teacher can usefully model an approach to such an activity where the initial focus is on the nature of the 'fillers' (noun, verb, adjective, etc) followed by considering the structure of the gapped sentences – 'what part of speech would fit syntactically?'.

This may be all the work that the teacher wants to do with some texts. Equally, if it is felt useful to do more intensive work it is worth considering different classroom organisation.

Intensive reading 2: Group work – jigsaw activity

Pupils working in groups of three or four can focus on one section of text, as allocated by the teacher. In order to reinforce the work already done, the activity could be similar to the above – a second gapped activity. For those who finish quickly they could themselves choose another section to work on. Other valid activities can follow. Pupils could devise:

- an assessment task for the rest of the class on their sections (e.g. multiple choice, true/false);
- a syntactically improved version (add any missing verbs, articles, etc);
- a similar type of brochure for their own area;
- a translation into English of their section.

Feedback from group work

Feedback can, but does not always have to be, to the whole class. Representatives from each group could form into new groups, to share the work they have done. This allows for more participation from more pupils.

The example in the text given above is from a standard Key Stage 3 text designed for Year 8 and 9 learners. Such a generic technique can be used effectively with longer, more demanding texts, particularly at Key Stage 4 GCSE Reading Higher Level and even AS and A Level as a 'way in'. Many able learners, even after several years of language learning, can be daunted by dense pages of text. This method of working can guide the pupils into a text, retaining their confidence, encouraging them to look at the text again and again from different angles, and not necessarily to feel that every single word has to be understood.

EXAMPLE 2

Generic Internet texts: Challenging subject matter; developing cultural awareness

The Internet can now provide quick access to topical material such as news (international, domestic, sports, etc) through all the major search engines. Downloading the day's headlines is not a lengthy process and it is something that many pupils themselves could do. In the following example the headlines have been copied into a standard Word document where they can then be edited. The editing consists of selecting a variety of headlines with an appropriate layout size and font. In the examples on pages 62 and 63 the language of the headlines is deliberately not altered or simplified.

Exploitation of authentic material

Material such as the news headlines could be given to the learners in the form of a worksheet but there are many alternative ways of presenting it (e.g. on an OHT; each headline on separate A4 sheets displayed round the classroom; PowerPoint presentation of 'running news' each headline appearing for a few seconds in a slide show).

Les actualités

1. Le Français tué en Arabie saoudite est originaire de la Vienne

2. Bertrand Cantat de retour en France mardi

3. Gard: évacuation d'une clinique située près d'un terril en combustion

4. Démantèlement d'un réseau de mariages blancs entre Saint-Etienne et Londres

5. Un garde du corps d'un des fils Kadhafi jugé pour coups et blessures

6. Renvoi du procès en appel d'Abdelhamid Hakkar pour le meurtre d'un policier

7. Rentrée universitaire: difficultés sociales et harmonisation des diplômes

8. Deux caïds présumés de la drogue jugés à Aix

9. Jeanne fait de nouveau des morts en Floride

10. Vaccin contre l'hépatite B: dépôt d'une plainte contre trois ministres de la Santé

Kurzberichte

1. Trauerfeier für Jassir Arafat in Kairo begonnen

2. Olympia kostet Griechenland fast neun Milliarden Euro

3. 16-Jährige wegen Verdachts auf Drogenschmuggel in Türkei vor Gericht

4. US-Armee in Falludscha offenbar kurz vor dem Ziel

5. 16 Tote und hundert Verletzte durch Erdbeben in Indonesien

6. 35-Jähriger erschießt vier Menschen und stellt sich der Polizei

7. Fünf Schiffe bei dichtem Nebel auf dem Rhein kollidiert

8. Jackson-Fans demonstrieren gegen Eminem-Video

9. Mindestens sechs Tote nach Erdbeben in Indonesien

10. Britischer Premier Blair zu Gast im Weißen Haus

1. El vuelco de un camión en la AP-7 en Castellón obliga a cortar dos carriles de la autopista y provoca retenciones

2. Reunión tripartita sobre Gibraltar en Kent

3. El Gobierno baraja que futbolistas famosos se involucren en la campaña sobre la Constitución Europea

4. Ulster. – Blair afirma que los esfuerzos para reactivas el proceso de paz en Ulster son 'notables pero aún incompletos'

5. Ucrania. – El mediador ruso en la crisis ucraniana califica de 'ilegal' la decisión del Supremo de repetir las elecciones

6. O. Próximo. – Un alto mando militar israelí reconoce que el Ejército mató este año a 148 civiles palestinos en Cisjordania

7. 'El Egipcio' será confinado en una celda de aislamiento pero con posibilidad de recibir visitas del exterior

8. Mueren tres jóvenes de 30, 25 y 22 años en una colisión frontal entre dos turismos en Abéjar (Soria)

9. Sanz lamenta 'la espiral de violencia' de ETA y defiende el Pacto por las Libertades para acabar con el terrorismo

10. Piden la máxima pena por asesinato para el hombre que mató en Córdoba a su ex pareja rociándola con ácido inflamable

Too difficult? Irrelevant?

The main challenges in the MFL classroom with authentic material will be that the language appears too complex, and often that the subject matter may not appear to be of immediate interest to the learners. Conversely it is important that our learners do develop a feel for the country they are studying as it exists at present, and that they become culturally aware. Equally, complex, 'difficult looking' language can raise the status of the activity (and the subject) if learners of all abilities are shown how they can positively respond to it.

Confidence boosting tasks

Confidence boosting tasks should initially avoid focussing on the meaning of every word but rather encourage the learners to scan the whole 'text'. Such tasks can include:

- quick word challenges;
- gist comprehension
- sentence work.

Quick word challenges

• Find names of people/places.
• How many times does one particular word occur?
• How many words look like English?

What strategies for pronunciation of such words can the pupils develop?

Gist comprehension

• Short English 'headlines' to create a matching exercise.
• Generic who? when? where? what? how? questions.
• Prioritising the items in pupils' own order of importance.

Sentence work

Headlines are often not complete sentences (it is common to find that definite/indefinite articles or finite verbs are omitted). Specific work dealing with the meaning and the structure of the headlines could be to reduce them down to their core meaning by identifying the most important four words in terms of meaning in any headline (i.e. create a snappy billboard headline). Using the headlines on pages 62 and 63, examples might look like this:

These could then be expanded into syntactically complete sentences (verbs, articles, etc). For example:

Le **Français** qui a été **tué** en Arabie saoudite est originaire de la Vienne

La **rentrée universitaire:** il y a des **difficultés sociales** et on va harmoniser des diplômes

Links with other skills

There are many ways in which such language can be reinforced in other skill areas:

- an audio tape of (some of) the headlines in a different order, with or without changes/omissions to the information – all of these can provide challenging combined listening and reading tasks;
- a speaking presentation (audio or video) as a twenty-second news bulletin where pupils choose some of the headlines and order them, adapting or simplifying the language as appropriate to their ability;
- using the language as the basis for a newspaper/newssheet;
- writing a personal diary of important events in the country over time, e.g. a whole year;
- developing a class map display of where incidents occurred with brief commentaries;
- a PowerPoint presentation of the headlines as a slide-show: this can provide an unusual reading challenge 'in time' – each headline only appears for a few seconds (but will come back). This can create a real sense of challenge in the class reading activity, as pupils have to attempt to remember text seen only for a limited period of time. It can offer an alternative to reading that is always paper-based.

EXAMPLE 3

Repeating short texts – focus on meaning; variety of language

The nature of reading texts even in the learner's own first language is changing. Many publications, particularly in the media, have re-thought the way they present information. Our learners are now more accustomed to text in shorter blocks, with more emphasis on the layout and the presentation. Comment pages in magazines and on Web pages can offer a variety of issues of concern to young people, written by young people from the country. The teacher may need to moderate/edit such texts for acceptable content and accuracy of the language.

The example on the following page is an **edited version** taken from the forum page on **www.momes.net**. This text dealing with the issues of extortion is one that most learners could probably identify with, even if they have not had direct experience of the problem. Possible activities are suggested below.

Initial gist whole-text reading

This could focus on the different types of contributors. What sort of contributors would you expect on such a page? Where possible pupils themselves could brainstorm the categories, for example:

- victims of extortion;
- witnesses of extortion – offering advice;
- a friend of a victim;
- adults offering advice.

Que pensez-vous du racket [taxage] à l'école, au collège? Que faut-il faire?

1. la première chose que je fais c'est en parler

2. prévenir quelqu'un est la meilleure des choses prendre son ami et le consoler

3. il FAUT que tu portes plainte contre elle

4. j'ai porté plainte contre le garçon qui m'a racketté

5. Bonjour, je travaille dans la police à Bruxelles. Tout projet en cours ou information utile sur ce genre de violence est la bienvenue

6. Je trouve aucun moyen d'y échapper

7. mettre la police à la sortie de chaque établissement scolaire

8. Ces agresseurs veulent montrer leur stupide supériorité!

9. Et si on développait dans l'école et dans sa classe des pratiques de solidarité

10. Il devrait y avoir plus de policiers devant les sorties d'écoles, de collèges, de lycées

11. C'est une forme de jalousie

12. Les agresseurs ont le plus souvent des problèmes familiaux et sociaux et veulent se venger sur ceux qui vivent bien

13. dites-le tout de suite à vos parents

14. tous ceux qui ont été victimes doivent en parler

15. Il faut le dire à nos parents

16. il vaut mieux rien apporter à l'école

Further gist 'text' level tasks

- Classifying and prioritising the types of incidents (any examples more serious than others?).
- Advice (practical/unrealistic) and the number of times mentioned.
- Reasons/causes.

Language development

Such a text provides a considerable variety of language around the same subject. Pupils could collect examples of:

• different ways the word 'racket' is used (noun/verb/active/passive/tenses);
• the language of 'advice';
• the language of opinions.

Links with other skills

As with the example of the newspaper headlines above a writing/editing task is to edit or summarise the language. If done using IT this can be a 'cutting' task.

Written reactions could include:

• reactions to the text/advice – *je suis d'accord/je ne ferais pas ça*;
• descriptions of any incidents from their own experience in French;
• comparisons with their own experience of the problem – *je pense que c'est mieux/pire ici en Angleterre parce que ... ;*

Although these suggestions might appear somewhat ambitious for some learners, judicious use of writing frames and structured sentences can allow learners over a wide range of ability to deal and respond to material that is of real interest to them.

In this and previous examples the teacher is the moderator who knows his or her learners and it might be decided to use fewer examples.

EXAMPLE 4

Use of text for reading comprehension and creative writing

The text on page 68, based on an article in a German tabloid newspaper, gives information about the German TV series Big Brother. The first task, *Lesen 1* is a standard multiple choice task such as will be encountered in any public examination. A standard technique to help pupils prepare for such tasks is to encourage them to look at the questions first and as far as possible make rational predictions. Once the first task has been completed, they are asked to use the language they have encountered as a basis for writing.

The second task, *Schreiben 2,* therefore challenges the learners to write creatively, in the style of a popular newspaper. To help, they are advised to look again not only at the language of the text but, more importantly, the language of the multiple choice questions. By choosing the 'worst', least likely answer they will then have the basis of a suitably exaggerated piece of journalism that gets all the facts wrong. This can be an effective task for learners of differing abilities. As well as having a clearly identifiable framework as a starting point for all, it can still allow more able learners considerable scope to be creative by adding more details and expressing an increasing sense of outrage!

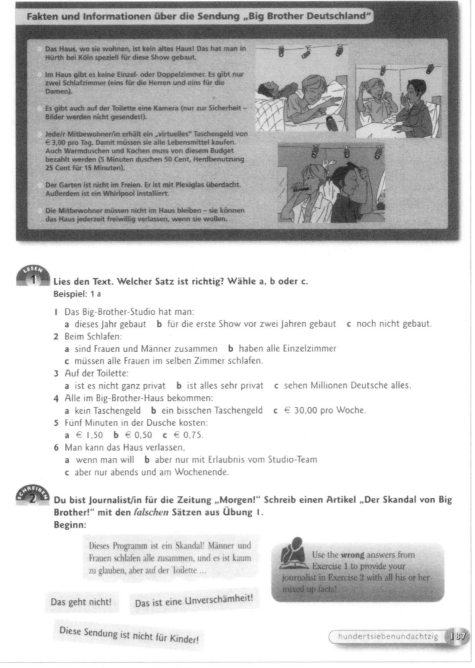

Fakten und Informationen über die Sendung „Big Brother Deutschland"

- Das Haus, wo sie wohnen, ist kein altes Haus! Das hat man in Hürth bei Köln speziell für diese Show gebaut.

- Im Haus gibt es keine Einzel- oder Doppelzimmer. Es gibt nur zwei Schlafzimmer (eins für die Herren und eins für die Damen).

- Es gibt auch auf der Toilette eine Kamera (nur zur Sicherheit – Bilder werden nicht gesendet!).

- Jede/r Mitbewohner/in erhält ein „virtuelles" Taschengeld von € 3,00 pro Tag. Damit müssen sie alle Lebensmittel kaufen. Auch Warmduschen und Kochen muss von diesem Budget bezahlt werden (5 Minuten duschen 50 Cent, Herdbenutzung 25 Cent für 15 Minuten).

- Der Garten ist nicht im Freien. Er ist mit Plexiglas überdacht. Außerdem ist ein Whirlpool installiert.

- Die Mitbewohner müssen nicht im Haus bleiben – sie können das Haus jederzeit freiwillig verlassen, wenn sie wollen.

1 **Lies den Text. Welcher Satz ist richtig? Wähle a, b oder c.**
Beispiel: 1 a

I Das Big-Brother-Studio hat man:
   a dieses Jahr gebaut   **b** für die erste Show vor zwei Jahren gebaut   **c** noch nicht gebaut.
2 Beim Schlafen:
   a sind Frauen und Männer zusammen   **b** haben alle Einzelzimmer
   c müssen alle Frauen im selben Zimmer schlafen.
3 Auf der Toilette:
   a ist es nicht ganz privat   **b** ist alles sehr privat   **c** sehen Millionen Deutsche alles.
4 Alle im Big-Brother-Haus bekommen:
   a kein Taschengeld   **b** ein bisschen Taschengeld   **c** € 30,00 pro Woche.
5 Fünf Minuten in der Dusche kosten:
   a € 1,50   **b** € 0,50   **c** € 0,75.
6 Man kann das Haus verlassen,
   a wenn man will   **b** aber nur mit Erlaubnis vom Studio-Team
   c aber nur abends und am Wochenende.

2 **Du bist Journalist/in für die Zeitung „Morgen!" Schreib einen Artikel „Der Skandal von Big Brother!" mit den *falschen* Sätzen aus Übung I.**
Beginn:

Dieses Programm ist ein Skandal! Männer und Frauen schlafen alle zusammen, und es ist kaum zu glauben, aber auf der Toilette ...

Use the **wrong** answers from Exercise 1 to provide your journalist in Exercise 2 with all his or her mixed up facts!

Das geht nicht!   Das ist eine Unverschämtheit!

Diese Sendung ist nicht für Kinder!

Source: *Logo 4 Rot*. Heinemann (Gray 2001)

EXAMPLE 5

Grabbing the pupils' interest – words can be texts

The realia above is an extract from of a collaboration between the Robert dictionary and *Libération* newspaper, highlighting new words that have emerged in French during the 1980s and 1990s. It is not a text in the usual sense. There are no sentences, or traditional paragraphs. Some of the language may seem too technical and certainly some of the vocabulary would tax many native speakers. Predictably the issue of the increasing amount of Anglo-Americanisms in French (as in all European languages) is also present.

However all of these concerns can be viewed positively and can offer a starting point for a variety of activities that can engage many of our learners who may lack interest in more traditional texts.

The following worksheet illustrates some possible strategies that could be used with such a text. They include:

- recognising cognates (and *faux amis*);
- French v. English spelling;
- pronunciation of cognates *à la française*;
- meaning of words – patterns, parts of speech;
- gist of 'texts' (made up of words instead of sentences);
- higher thinking skills (use of *verlan*);
- 'world knowledge' of other languages;
- identifying and using frequent sentence pattern (e.g. definitions).

Les nouveaux mots en français – les années 80/90

Il y a combien de mots internationaux?
Le même en français et en anglais?

C'est presque le même en anglais!
Comment ça s'écrit en anglais?

… des années 90 …

- émoticone
- nanotechnologie
- politiquement correct
- portail
- armes de destruction massive
- pin's

… des années 80 …

- tchatcher
- vidéosurveillance
- dopeur
- sampler
- rapper

Peux-tu en trouver d'autres exemples?

Mais qu'est-ce que c'est?

- téléachat
- télépéage
- vidéaste
- rafting
- planchiste
- badger

Les grands thèmes. Cherche les groupes de mots pour chaque thème!

- les loisirs
- la culture des jeunes dans les villes
- à la maison
- la musique
- l'informatique
- les problèmes de la vie urbaine
- l'environnement
- la cuisine
- la politique
- la vie des jeunes alternative

C'est qui?

- quelqu'un qui fait du vélo
- quelqu'un qui joue au rugby
- quelqu'un qui fait de la planche à voile

Peux-tu continuer la liste?
Un .... est quelqu'un qui
aime/adore ....

Qu'est-ce que c'est? Des définitions …

a pacser
b dégraffitage
c internaute
d malbouffe
e VTT

1 la cuisine qui n'est pas bonne pour la santé!
2 un moyen de transport très pratique, à la campagne, à la montagne
3 faire un contrat (entre deux personnes, pareil au mariage)
4 nettoyer les murs des villes
5 quelqu'un qui adore l'Internet

C'est quoi exactement …

une teuf?
- une personne violente
- une fête

le pacs?
- un contrat comme le mariage
- faire un contrat comme le mariage

une meuf?
- une femme
- une mauvaise personne

kifer?
- plaire
- couper

à donf?
- à fond
- comme donation

Il y un mot français pour …

- *e-mail?*
- *search engine?*
- *to host (a website)?*

Il y a beaucoup de mots anglo-américains en français. Mais il y a aussi quelques exemples d'autres langues par exemple le japonais, l'italien. Cherche des exemples!

Differentiated tasks

As these tasks suggest they can be used with learners of different levels of ability. Not all pupils may do all tasks but there is scope for differentiation. Ideally the teacher would model (some of) the different tasks (and not necessarily in traditional order, from top left to bottom right). As a base line, learners could be asked to choose any four of the eight activities to complete, in any order, within a given time. The extension task could then be to complete as many of the other tasks as possible. This way of working allows individuals to have some control over how they work and to choose what interests them. It also helps deal with the problem of when an activity should end. What otherwise do those who finish quickly then do? How demotivating is it for a slower learner never to complete the task set?

Motivating the learners

The text is in many ways untraditional – it does not look like a traditional text and it is about topics where even the teacher may feel uncertain (and learn something new!). However all of this may appeal to many of the learners in our classroom. The content may even be more familiar to learners, especially in the area of cognates, than to the teacher. Crucially it deals with the modern, globalising world in a way in which many traditional texts fall short.

EXAMPLE 6

Exploiting 'pre-knowledge': What do our learners bring to texts?

Readers come to stories with all sorts of expectations of what is possible in terms of types of character, settings and possible storylines. One particularly useful piece of information for language learners, for example, is that if they already know the story in their own language they will be aware of the overall structure and maybe even some key words.

The original starting point for the following activity was material written by foreign language assistants. They had been asked to write short versions of different fairy stories. They produced a number of different versions of the same story.

To prepare the pupils they were given a sheet containing jumbled key words and titles from three different stories (see page 72). They had to decide what words fitted with which story (doing as much as they could initially without, and then with, the aid of dictionaries).

Having agreed as a class on the sorting of these three categories the next task was to arrange these words in the order in which they would occur in the story. The pupils then had to add four more key words of their own that they thought might appear.

As there were a minimum of five versions of each complete story, pupils were able to read at least some of them and make comparisons between them and with their own original predictions.

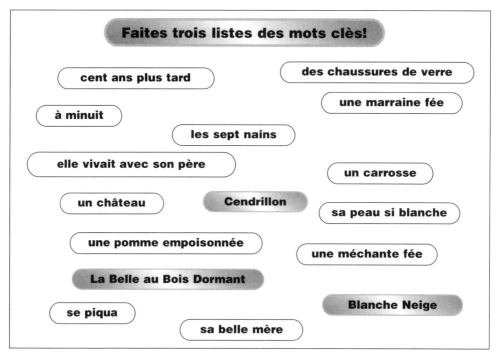

Faites trois listes des mots clès!

cent ans plus tard

des chaussures de verre

une marraine fée

à minuit

les sept nains

elle vivait avec son père

un carrosse

un château

Cendrillon

sa peau si blanche

une pomme empoisonnée

une méchante fée

La Belle au Bois Dormant

Blanche Neige

se piqua

sa belle mère

Another more open-ended activity is to brainstorm with pupils the types of words they might encounter in the text. Versions written by the assistants have also provided a useful stepping stone to 'real French' versions, such as the *Contes* by Perrault.

No pre-knowledge?

Apart from this specific example of fairy tales, pre-knowledge of most stories will be unlikely but a simple checklist completed in advance could encourage pupils to think about how a story might develop:

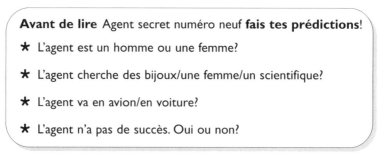

Avant de lire Agent secret numéro neuf **fais tes prédictions**!

★ L'agent est un homme ou une femme?

★ L'agent cherche des bijoux/une femme/un scientifique?

★ L'agent va en avion/en voiture?

★ L'agent n'a pas de succès. Oui ou non?

As well as questions specific to a particular story, there are also generic questions that can be used when reading any story, such as:

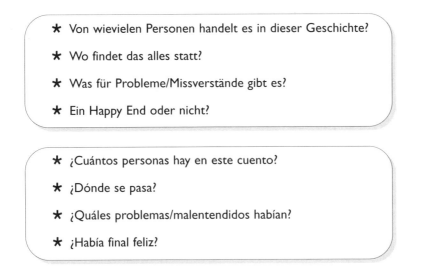

★ Von wievielen Personen handelt es in dieser Geschichte?

★ Wo findet das alles statt?

★ Was für Probleme/Missverstände gibt es?

★ Ein Happy End oder nicht?

★ ¿Cuántos personas hay en este cuento?

★ ¿Dónde se pasa?

★ ¿Quáles problemas/malentendidos habían?

★ ¿Había final feliz?

Pre-knowledge of factual texts may sometimes exist, even if only partially and/or inaccurately. Before reading a text about, for example, the differences between schools in France and England, pupils could look at this list and make their own decisions about which apply to which country. They then compare their predictions with what the writer feels, deciding at the same time whether they disagree with anything the writer has said.

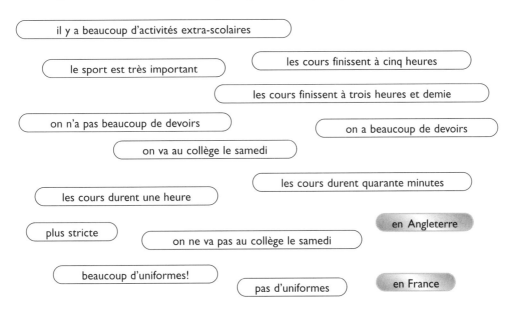

il y a beaucoup d'activités extra-scolaires

le sport est très important

les cours finissent à cinq heures

les cours finissent à trois heures et demie

on n'a pas beaucoup de devoirs

on a beaucoup de devoirs

on va au collège le samedi

les cours durent quarante minutes

les cours durent une heure

plus stricte

on ne va pas au collège le samedi

en Angleterre

beaucoup d'uniformes!

pas d'uniformes

en France

1 En France, à l'école, les élèves étudient toutes les matières comme base générale. (français, histoire, géographie, mathématiques, sciences physiques/naturelles, éducation physique, anglais)

2 En France, les élèves ont plus d'heures de cours dans la journée, environ 7 heures.

3 En France, il y a deux récréations. Une le matin vers 10h 15mn, une l'après-midi vers 15h.

4. En France, les élèves ne portent pas d'uniforme.

5. En France, les élèves ont des feuilles de papier à carreaux.

6. En France, les notes sont importantes pour le passage dans la classe supérieure.

7. En France, si un élève ne travaille pas bien, il redouble sa classe.

8. En France, l'école finit à 17h.

9. En France, les élèves étudient la grammaire anglaise ou allemande ou espagnole.

10. En France, les élèves remmènent leurs livres. Leurs cartables sont lourds.

WHY WAS A TEXT WRITTEN?

The examples of texts looked at so far cover a range of factual and imaginative writing. Although it may seem too sophisticated a discussion to have in the foreign language, it is also worth asking pupils to consider **why** the text was actually written.

Having done a variety of extensive and intensive exercises on a tourist brochure with a Year 10 group, a final task was to consider who would have written it and how this would have affected the way it was written. Having established that the writer of a tourist brochure would want visitors to come to the area described, pupils then managed to identify some of the ways in which the writer was trying to achieve this. Use of superlative adjectives, phrases like *weltberühmt* (world famous) and positive references to the weather were all identified.

3 Developing a policy for independent reading

The concern to encourage pupils to read independently is not new. Indeed, the presence of dusty readers from the sixties in stock cupboards throughout the country bears witness to this. As William Rowlinson pointed out:

> *Ideas ... have a habit of coming into and going out of fashion. What is taught and how it is taught is a product of these ideas, as well as of the conditions in which it is to be taught ... many, perhaps most, new approaches are rediscoveries of old methods neglected and left in the shade, now re-illuminated by the light of social need.* (Rowlinson 1985)

Independent reading is a case in point. Encouraged by the introduction of the National Curriculum, MFL departments are keen for their pupils to develop their independence as linguists, and reading plays a central part in this development, as Grenfell suggests:

> *It is, after all, the least inhibiting of the four skills; the most comfortable to work with. Pupils can work at their own pace, reading, re-reading, checking and responding with their own thought patterns. At the very least this frees lessons from over-domination by the teacher.* (Grenfell 1992)

In departments where independent reading has become a priority, it is common to find that a reading policy has been drawn up to ensure that all pupils have equal access to books and equal opportunity to read independently. The provision differs from school to school. Some provide a mobile bank of different texts for pupils and staff to use when needed, while others have set up systematised reading schemes situated in the school library or in a dedicated languages room.

SETTING UP AN INDEPENDENT READING SCHEME

There are practical issues beyond the availability and provision of suitable texts which need to be addressed if a department is considering setting up a reading scheme. Issues range from how structured the scheme should be to how much monitoring will be required by the teacher, to the link between independent reading and other classroom activities, and to the need for a programme of developing reading skills in general. Other issues which need to be discussed are:

- the amount of teacher involvement required during an independent reading lesson;
- access to dictionaries;

- whether there should be multiple copies of popular books available;
- where the books should be housed (in the school library or in a classroom or on a trolley);
- whether books should be on loan;
- whether there should be scheduled reading periods;
- whether there might be a reading club;
- what access there can be to the Internet during and outside class time;
- how a list of recommended websites can be developed;
- how learners can be encouraged to recommend websites they have discovered themselves;
- whether pupils should be set targets (e.g. to read at least one book and one magazine per term);
- what titles should be provided (the balance between fiction and non-fiction);
- whether pupils should complete comprehension exercises after finishing a book;
- whether pupils should keep a record of what they have read;
- the storage system;
- how to provide a regular, recent selection of newspapers and a selection of specialist young people's magazines (ICT, sport, music).

Once these issues have been resolved, then a department might move towards drawing up a reading policy. Such a policy could look something like the example below.

The independent reading programme

References to the National Curriculum Programme of Study

2h ... techniques for skimming and scanning written texts for information, including those from ICT-based sources

3b ... how to use context and other clues to establish meaning

3d ... how to use dictionaries and other reference materials appropriately and effectively

3e how to develop their independence in learning and using the target language

4a ... (to work) with authentic materials in the target language, including some from ICT-based sources

5g ... (read) for personal interest and enjoyment, as well as for information

References to the Key Stage 3 Strategy

The following objectives are selected from Strand 3 (Text Level):

7T1 How to read and understand simple texts using cues in language, layout and context to aid understanding

8T3 To begin to associate aspects of language with different text types

9T1 How to use their knowledge of context and grammar to understand texts involving complex grammar

The main elements of the independent reading programme consist of the reading box and a structured reading period. Beyond this, the choice of material must be considered along with the use of reference material and building in tasks.

The reading box

For each year there is a **reading box** which will contain a variety of material appropriate to the year.

The Internet

For each year there are recommended sites and generic questions for pupils to enable them to write brief summaries of what they have discovered.

A reading period

In order to raise the profile of such reading, and to establish good habits, it is suggested that each class should have:

- a regular, timetabled **30-minute reading session** once a fortnight – teachers will need to **book** the **reading box** and a set of dictionaries for this half period;
- timetabled access to the Internet during and outside class time and with encouragement for pupils to 'book themselves in'.

Choice of books, magazines and websites

Each box is structured with the ability of the pupils in mind. Teachers will, however, need to offer some guidance to pupils so that they do not make unrealistic choices and become disillusioned.

The teacher's role

During reading periods, reading from books or from the screen should be the main activity, i.e. the material should not be treated as something for the rest to do while the teacher does 'x, y or z' with individual pupils and it would, of course, help if the teacher models the example as well by reading for at least some of the time.

'What does this mean?' Using reference material

Only some of the material will contain word lists, so it will be necessary for pupils to become familiar with the use of dictionaries. Pupils need to be reminded that there are other ways of discovering meaning – seeing if it looks like an English word, saying it, checking their own vocabulary lists, asking a neighbour or someone who has already read the book, possibly the assistant and even occasionally, as a last resort, the teacher. Teachers might want to establish a series of steps: 'before you do this … '.

Tasks and diaries

One of the aims must be to maintain a balance between reading and tasks on the reading, as there can be a danger that pupils spend more time on the exercises than on reading. The tasks need to be kept in perspective, although one task that pupils should **always** do is to record a small number, four or five, new words they have come across, along with their meaning.

Other generic tasks that can easily be used with any material include:

- brief summaries;
- predictions about what will happen – how accurate were you?;
- making a cast list of all the people in the story;
- listing scenes/props needed for a film version;
- acting out/recording a very brief episode from a book, changing/adapting language.

Factual material

Such material on the culture of the country may be more useful for Key Stage 4 pupils in linking with work on GCSE topics. Some generic activities that can work are, for example, having a class collection of interesting facts culled from these sources and possible links with IT.

Book week

The reading period will not be appropriate for Year 7 pupils at the beginning of their course, but in October all Year 7 pupils will have the material presented to them in a high profile exercise involving displays, library work and presentations by older pupils of individual books.

Setting targets

The teacher will need to decide what are realistic targets for pupils but it may be worth stating that 'during the term/year everybody should have read at least **x** number of books and looked at **y** number of sites'. Pupils could also, after some time, be asked to select one book or site they have particularly enjoyed and to return to it and do some in-depth work on it. This could include devising activities for other readers, a poster recommending it, a short oral presentation to the class or to younger pupils (see above Year 7 – Book week) or a survey of what other people thought of it.

READING DIARIES

Where reading has become an important part of life in the languages classroom it is sometimes considered valuable for pupils to record what they have read in a reading diary. This provides the opportunity for pupils to reflect upon what they have read and to record their achievements. The diaries are usually records of pupils' independent reading or web surfing and may take a very flexible format, where the date is recorded together with a summary of what has been read – maybe forming part of an exercise book.

THE DIARY AS A DIALOGUE

Another model of a reading diary might take the form of a written dialogue between teacher and pupils where the pupil jots down impressions, interesting points and problems as they occur. The teacher then writes a reply in the diary. This form of diary may be more suitable for post-16 pupils tackling more sophisticated texts who will be studying in more depth than those lower down the school. One such system, designed to develop critical reading skills, is described by Gabrielle Cliff Hodges (Homerton College, Cambridge) below. Though the 'reading journal' described is for pupils of English, there are many messages for language teachers. Whether the journal is kept in the foreign language or English would be an issue to be discussed and decided by teacher and pupils together:

> *The value of using journals lies in pupils recording in some detail their initial encounters with texts rather than solely their final ideas and opinions. Pupils' journals thus include dated entries made at various stages before, during and after the reading of a text [...] What it provides [...] is a continuous record of reading of all kinds. The entries also form one side of a dialogue with the teacher about both the text and the processes of reading it [...] Although time is required on the part of the teacher for reading and responding to journal entries, it is also worth bearing in mind that pupils will neither want, nor will they need, to write one on every occasion they do some reading.* (Cliff Hodges 1994)

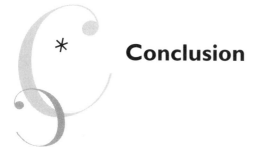

Conclusion

In the last ten years many features on the educational landscape have changed. Thanks to the *National Literacy Strategy* and the *KS3 Strategy*, in all areas of the curriculum there is now greater awareness of the need to focus on the nature of language. Learners need to be equipped with an understanding of language if they are to use it to interpret information and communicate their own ideas. One of the main issues for MFL teachers is to ensure that this general awareness is reinforced and that at the same time the specific demands of second language learning are also met. The MFL teacher needs to plan how a variety of types of text can be seen as central to learning, and how to encourage learners of all abilities to rise to the challenge. Advances in technology, in particular the development of the Internet, offer a whole new dimension to our teaching.

We, as language teachers, have a vast and rich resource in the literature and authentic texts of our target cultures. But we need to develop our own interest in that culture by reading as widely as we can and by communicating that interest to our pupils. We ourselves need to be seen as enthusiastic and committed readers so that we become role models to our pupils. It may prove true that the reading habit can be contagious.

> *Reading is like an infectious disease; it is caught, not taught. (And you can't catch it from someone who hasn't got it.)* (Nuttall 1982)

But we have learnt in the years since the first edition of this Pathfinder, and since the re-emergence of interest in independent reading, that motivating pupils to read and providing texts which they will enjoy does not fully equip them to develop their independence. We need also to think about explicitly teaching them strategies to use when meeting an unfamiliar text for the first time. In this way reading can become an exciting and enriching experience for pupils. We hope that this Classic Pathfinder will go some way towards supporting you in your task.

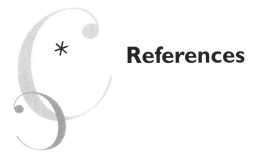

References

Department for Education and Skills (2003) *Key Stage 3 National Strategy. Framework for teaching Modern Foreign Languages: Years 7, 8 and 9*. HMSO.

DfES (1998) *The National Literacy Strategy – Framework for teaching*. HMSO.

Cliff Hodges, G. (1994) *A rest from Shakespeare – developing independent reading in the secondary school*. National Association for the teaching of English – 12–16 Committee.

Giles Jones, M. (1998) 'Reading – the poor relation – report of a modem languages in-service course'. In: *The British Journal of Language Teaching*, vol 26, no. 2, Autumn 1988.

Grenfell, M. (1992) 'Reading and communication in the modern languages classroom – perspectives on reading'. In: *Centre for Languages Education Working Papers*, no. 2. University of Southampton.

Les années 80/90. Liberation/Robert.

Gray, C. (2001) *Logo 4 rot*. Heinemann.

McNab, R. (2002) *Métro 3 rouge*. Heinemann.

Nuttall, C. (1982) *Teaching reading skills in a foreign language*. Heinemann Educational.

Rowlinson, W. (1985) *Personally speaking – teaching languages for use*. Oxford University Press.

 ## WEBSITES

www.momes.net/forum
www.olympiade.de